THE
PROVENÇAL HOUSE

Published by
Stewart, Tabori & Chang
A Company of La Martinière Groupe
115 West 18th Street
New York, NY 10011

Canadian Distribution:
Canadian Manda Group
One Atlantic Avenue, Suite 105
Toronto, Ontario M6K 3E7
Canada

Library of Congress Cataloguing-in-Publication Data
Thornycroft, Johanna.
    The Provençal house / Johanna Thornycroft and Andreas von Einsiedel.
      p. cm.
    Includes bibliographical references and index.
    ISBN 1-58479-310-4
1. Provence (France)-Social life and customs-Pictorial works.
2. Provence (France)-Description and travel-Pictorial works.
3. Dwellings-France-Provence-Pictorial works.
4. Architecture, Domestic-France-Provence-Pictorial works.
5. Interior decoration-France-Provence-Pictorial works.
6. Lifestyles-France-Provence-Pictorial works.
      I. Einsiedel, Andreas. II. Title.

DC 611.P958T49 2003
728'.37'09449022-dc21   2003045855

The text of this book was composed in Indispose typeface.

Designer Karen Watts

Printed in Italy.

10 9 8 7 6 5 4 3 2 1
First U.S. Printing

THE
PROVENÇAL HOUSE

WRITTEN BY JOHANNA THORNYCROFT AND
PHOTOGRAPHED BY ANDREAS VON EINSIEDEL

stewart tabori & chang
New York

Contents

THE TOWN HOUSE   10

Rue de L'Eglise   12
Kismet   28
Rue du Maupas   46

THE MANOR HOUSE   60

Pavillon de Victoire   62
Les Mas du Grès   80
Domaine du Grand Cros   102

THE COUNTRY HOUSE   120

Les Maccans   122
Mas du Manescau   136
Les Bas Artèmes   154
La Bergerie du Bosquet   170
Les Mas de L'Esquières   184
Le Murier   198

Index   215
Acknowledgments   216

Much has been written about Provence - the most visited and acclaimed region of France - so it is surprising to find that people still disagree about where the ancient province begins and ends. Its boundaries, which moved constantly throughout centuries of invasion, were fixed in 1947, so geographically speaking it lies between Italy in the east, and beyond the great waterway of the Rhône to the west. Yet, to many Parisians their Provence (the real Provence) is a 'golden triangle' from Avignon and Arles to Aix-en-Provence and nominally the westerly side of the Lubéron. There is passion and possession in every argument, and for all Provençaux - and, indeed, recent arrivals - the boundaries will continue to expand and contract.

Although outwardly much changed by industry, tourism and highways, the essential unwavering attraction remains undiluted. Ringed by broken and often desolate mountain ranges, these ancient natural fortifications define the quality of light and vegetation and, along with the Durance and Rhône rivers, provided the protection, warmth and water that were (and largely still are to this day) the region's lifeblood, first agricultural and now touristic. Many smaller limestone ridges run east and west within the outer mountain ranges, and - though relatively easy to quarry - the pale, malleable stone has endured, defining Provençal architecture from the humble cabanon (country cottage) to the grand chateau. When the Romans incorporated the province into their vast administration some 2000 years ago, they began a tradition of quarrying that survives to this day.

Planners insist that new buildings echo the past, either in stone or painted stuccowork. The old elements of architecture remain and live on, be they gently sloping roofs covered in Roman tiles, traditional wooden shutters or limewash colors echoing the natural pigments of the earth. While in many parts of the world craftsmen have all but disappeared, Provence has retained and encouraged its ironworkers, who replicate the delicate window latches of the eighteenth century; its masons cut, carve and polish affordable stone floors and fireplaces; its fabric printers and potters flourish - millions of traditionally colored and sized tiles are produced every year; and dry-stone walling, so critical in supporting terraces of olives, fruit trees and vegetables, is often beautifully maintained.

While the earliest masons cut and shaped limestone blocks and carved superb classical details atop temple columns, their architects knew to beware of the mistral, the chill northwesterly wind that blows from the Massif Central. Fierce, and often penetratingly cold, it blows for days and sometimes weeks, exhausting the land and its inhabitants. Shattering nerves and flimsy structures, it is as important an influence on the Provençal house as the still, baking summers that can shock like the not-too-distant Sahara. The mistral and the shimmering, soporific heat are the great levellers that all human, animal and plant life has had to come to terms with. The largely blind, windowless north walls of rural mas or bastides (with their small doors and solid stone facades) present a cohesive defence against the elements. Details vary from *département to département,* as does the climate there is no need for such protection in the Alpes Maritimes, but then, is that Provence?

The evolution of Provençal architecture is one based on defence against people and the elements. There is evidence, for example, in cave dwellings that perhaps the descendants of the earliest human migrations from Africa lived along the Côte d'Azur. By late Neolithic times, the population had increased and the inhabitants had devised skills for building and creating settlements, which in turn required protection. Change and development was rapid. The transhumance began (the moving of sheep in summer from the lowlands to fresh grazing in the hills); forests were felled for timber and fuel; and the first roads, or rather trackways, were being used by farmers and traders. Before the Romans forged inland, the first *oppida* (primitive towns) were being built, defensive dry-stone walls and lookout posts appearing on strategic high ground.

From about 1000 BCE, Phoenicians, Greeks, Celts and Ligurians arrived by sea and from the north, leaving behind them numerous cultural, social and agricultural influences. The vine and the olive arrived and changed the face of Provence for ever. Little can be found today of these peoples, but for 600 years the Romans made the province their own, until the collapse of the western empire in CE 476. Superb public buildings, roads, aqueducts and bridges were built, vast areas of marshy ground were drained, and the area around Arles became as important to Rome for food production as the great grain-growing areas of the Nile delta. Much of what we see in Provence today was shaped by the Romans and, although Christianity brought great churches - forming the center of many communities - in the sixteenth century, Provence was still in the process of being converted. Roman architecture is still to be found from Fréjus to Arles, Aix-en-Provence, Nimes and Orange, attracting enormous numbers of tourists, who marvel at such early building skills.

Little remains of the period known as the Dark Ages, but the Middle Ages brought about renewed vigor and optimism. It is the stone-built medieval villages and the walled, hilltop towns that have survived (and latterly flourished), adding so much to the personality and appeal of Provence today. Renewal and renovation of both houses and gardens is being undertaken with almost religious zeal by an international coterie of owners. Interior decoration has changed, and one is more likely to find pure white minimal spaces, European designer furniture and antique Asian textiles than the layers of exuberant, hand-blocked cotton prints of the 1970s and 1980s. Provençal furniture is expensive and hard to find, so decoration has become more eclectic and certainly global, but the charm continues nonetheless.

THE TOWN HOUSE

Mougins

RUE DE L'ÉGLISE

Although the French Riviera is thought of as a magnet for summer visitors, film festivals and excess, it is an area of great geographical diversity, and just a few kilometers inland from the busy coast roads a surprisingly gentle, verdant landscape emerges. The great coastal resorts all but close during the winter - in contrast to the early days before World War I, when European, English and Russian aristocracy flocked to the south for the entire winter. Then the stifling heat of summer was unthinkable, but now attitudes have changed, the seasons are less important and the year-round population has brought regeneration and wealth to the interior.

The tiny fishing villages strung out along the rugged coastline have been submerged by grand hotels, towering apartment blocks and shopping centers that barely allude to French (let alone Provençal) architectural styles, but leave the Gulf of St Tropez or the madness of Cannes and suddenly the familiarity returns. Protected by the north-south folding of the Alpes Maritimes, the area is sheltered and warm. Flowers are grown for cutting and export, and for the perfume industry in Grasse, but imported exotics like dates, bananas and avocados also thrive. There is a softer face to the landscape here - greener, rounder hills and (of course) more people - but the old hill villages have come to life once more. Many, such as Gordes, which lies 150km (100 miles) further west, have been rebuilt by artists, musicians, painters and potters.

Like most early Provençal villages, Mougins was built on the top of a hill, with houses forming an outer protective ring. Narrow lanes between them were easily defended and stone gateways could be closed off when under threat. Walking up to the village today, it is possible to see the layers of development by the terrace-like roads on each level. Newer dwellings, shops and restaurants suddenly give way to a solid, cohesive wall of buildings that are embedded on solid rock. The lower floors are usually cut into the rock face and lined with stone vaulting, and it was here that the business of the house was conducted - from forge to feather-mattress maker, trade was carried on below the living quarters. This typical four-storied house is now home to antiques dealers, although they have recently moved the business from the house to a shop nearby. The ground floor remains much as it always was: cool, dimly lit and a place where one feels, quite literally, the weight of centuries of building above. Once more, regeneration came in the late twentieth century. Its south face is open to a panorama of wooded hills and tiled roofs, but the entrance is on the first floor via a medieval street that is barely wide enough for a bicycle. The two faces are in complete contrast.

The house (or, rather, its remnants) is 900 years old. Proof that it formed part of the early protective wall of the village was discovered after 150 tonnes (150 tons) of debris were removed during renovation, revealing internal doorways to both left and right. The village inhabitants, it seems, could move right round the perimeter of the village without actually having to take to the streets. Although a great deal of work has been carried out to restore the old house, it retains a remarkable sense of age and, again, it is testament to the sensitivity and care brought to the resuscitation of ancient dwellings by their most recent owners. Timber, lime-washed plaster and tiled floors set the scene. The interior decoration is all about

texture and subtle color. Unlike many village houses of the period, it is not a tall thin, column of a house; there is no tight staircase winding up the wall, but rather one that is generously wide, with shallow risers.

Again, unusually, there are small landings, off which two or three rooms lead. The old, vaulted shop below is used as a summer dining room - simply furnished with curtains made of woad-dyed sheeting, a country table, and painted chairs and chests. The first floor houses the kitchen and drawing room, both with yellow-ochre-washed walls. An old wooden lintel was discovered to the left of the entrance, so it was decided to reuse the old doorway as access to the new kitchen (built in Provençal style without slavishly trying to recreate a pastiche of the past). One half of the room serves as an informal dining area, with large windows overlooking the streets below.

The hall and staircase leading to the second floor have been colored in a pinky terracotta shade that leads to the pale-blue and white master bedroom and bathroom. Two pretty spare rooms are also housed on this floor and, on the top, part of the stairwall has been removed. This exposes a large, light space that is used as part-office, part-sitting room, with a further bedroom and bathroom attached. Further up - via a spiral staircase - there is a charming roof terrace. This seems higher than any other building around apart from the nearby church steeple, with its typical iron bell-

cage. For town and village dwellers, this terrace is the most valuable living space during summer: a place to feel the breeze, watch the uniquely Provençal sunsets and listen to the myriad sounds of the night.

Much of the furnishings in the house are French, although mixing period and style works well through the constant theme of using well-worn painted furniture and old fabric. It may have been tempting for the owners to fill the establishment with "Provençal style", but they have consciously left plenty of space to move around chairs, tables and beds, and have limited curtains and coverings to cottons and linen, printed, striped and plain. The exterior is perfect simplicity: its walls are plastered and painted a pale, creamy yellow, and the shutters (both back and front) are a soft olive green. Thick walls ensure a degree of quiet, but as always there is a strong sense of community as villagers greet one another through kitchen windows, on doorsteps or at the *boulangerie*. Few cars interfere with life here and, while constantly moving about on foot, the residents are conscious equally of their neighborhood and of one another.

LEFT

Mougins' medieval pedestrian streets are narrow, with houses tightly grouped along and within the old walls. Originally built 900 years ago, there is clear evidence here that - for defence - internal doors linked the dwellings.

OPPOSITE

A rustic old Provençal door leads to the cellar off the main salon. The walls have been colored with yellow ochre, which has been rubbed on to the plaster to create an aged finish.

LEFT

Typical full-length French windows open on to tiny wrought-iron balconies across the front of the house. Reclaimed nineteenth-century floor tiles have been laid throughout the reception rooms, providing a richly colored, cohesive backdrop to a fine collection of antique furniture and textiles.

ABOVE

One of several period stone fireplaces that were installed during extensive renovation work. Great care was taken with the choice of doors, fireplaces, bathrooms and decorative finishes, in order that the interior looked ageless and in keeping with the centuries-old house.

RUE DE L'ÉGLISE

OPPOSITE

The salon and adjoining kitchen take up the whole of the street-level ground floor. Lit by two pairs of French doors leading to tiny balconies, the south-facing rooms are furnished with an eclectic mix of Provençal and regional French furniture and mirrors. Blue and beige linens upholster the chairs and sofas.

ABOVE & OPPOSITE

Many a conversation takes place through the street-facing kitchen window. Running from the front to the back of the house, this living space includes an eight-seat fruitwood dining table and painted, rush-seated chairs. All the cupboards – including an enormous one for china – are painted in a distressed, soft olive green.

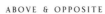

OPPOSITE & ABOVE

This view of the ground-level dining room (opposite), formerly a workshop, clearly shows how old houses were literally built into the village rock face and often expanded above over a long period of time. Lined with stone and lit only by a door to the street, the atmosphere hints at a secret cave dwelling. Many owners still run businesses from these ancient vaults, although now they are more likely to be selling linens than manufacturing them. Decorative metal window latches have changed little over 200 years, the cut-out designs varying from one dwelling to another.

ABOVE & LEFT

Pale blue predominates in the master bedroom. Walls are washed in the
lightest tone, antique toile and checked linen is used for cushions, and a
superb painted dresser with curved drawers is an ideal dressing table.
Original distressed paintwork like this is highly sought after worldwide.

OPPOSITE

Parts of the hall walls have been cut away, so allowing light to penetrate the
staircase as it rises to the top floor. Country chairs and a collection of
French oil paintings depicting nineteenth-century rural scenes are placed
on each of the landings.

LEFT & BELOW
This bedroom and bathroom leads off the room opposite. Decorated in pale colors, it is more feminine than the richly colored reception rooms, and is simply furnished with a painted metal bed and side-table. The elegant, although unadorned, curving canopy over the bed gives a sculptural aspect to the pretty wrought-iron work .

OPPOSITE
Soaring timber-beamed ceilings herald the top of the house, which is now opened up to form a spacious workroom and office. In the center is a spiral staircase leading to the roof terrace, and to the right is a guest bedroom decorated in feminine Provençal style.

KISMET

Arles was the Roman capital of Provence and a major religious center in the Middle Ages. Layer upon layer of history from as far back as 1000 BCE lies above and below its streets, testament to the importance and endurance of a settlement that sits astride the great Rhône waterway. It has the air of being the most Provençal of all the major towns and was once described as being "in sharp contrast with Avignon's pure feudalism, Aix's donnish reticence and Marseille's aggressive modernity".

To live in the center of Arles is to be at once immersed in ancient history (the Roman town grid is still recognizable, and both the theater and amphitheater are in constant use), and also to be surrounded by the region's most spectacular surviving hôtels particuliers (private mansions). The city has survived numerous outside influences, including ravishing bouts of the plague, but society (in those days, as it does today) loved to show off, and architecture was the best way for wealthy families to demonstrate their prestige within the community. Much communal property was sold off after the religious wars and the nobility started to build in the spirit of the Counter-Reformation. This house, on one of Arles most picturesque streets, has witnessed many changes during its religious and secular life: in around 1666, the Order of St Augustine was established in Arles and a convent was built, using stone from the Roman theater located a few strides away, silent since choirs gave voice to the Greek and Roman tragedies of Sophocles and Seneca, and the area reawakened to Christian chant. Records reveal that the house was called 'La Maison Lyon' in the early 1800s and was occupied by an antique-dealing priest - which is suitably amusing to the current owner, who also deals in antiques. It was about this time, not long after the French Revolution, that the street was realigned and renamed, and it has remained largely unchanged to this day.

Evidence of this change is seen only in the nineteenth-century entrance hall. The front door lines up with the street, but what is now the inner lobby is on a different line. No matter - for there is a distinct feeling of age already. The walls are 60cm (2ft) thick, the ceilings are high and show closely set timbers that are decorated with painted scroll and leaf patterns, conserved some years ago to reveal their original vivid red and blue colors. Nearly all town houses of this period had an interior courtyard and often it is here that the origins and certainly the oldest, untouched parts of these houses can be found. Arches and narrow stone corridors lead to blank walls, evidence of changing fortunes, fashions and remodeling. Typically, too, it was the ground floor that contained the most lavish reception room until fashion changed and it became common to furnish the first floor with the latest styles and fabrics.

Pale cream stone was chosen for the wide, shallow-stepped staircase that leads up the right-hand side of the house. Both architectural and sculptural, it is well worn, unadorned and lit by a single colored-glass window reminiscent of the monastic past. Like the ground floor, the first-floor drawing room wraps part-way around the central courtyard but has tiny wrought-iron balconies holding flowerpots and tall, unpainted, very old shutters. Both rooms contain fireplaces, each with the shell motif of Arles above the

mantel. Off the drawing room and facing the street is the very light kitchen, one end of which is tiled in rich green Provençal tiles set against highly polished terracotta floor tiles. The room is filled with wonderfully over-scaled furniture and a collection of pieces chosen simply for their presence. The dining table is made from a section of Provençal painted ceiling and above the sink stands a seventeenth-century Venetian gilded lion. Old Spanish window trellis breaks up the massive expanse of wall above, and filling the space between a pair of full-height windows is a giant, fruitwood draper's table from Lyon. Even the *Trinquetaille* glass vinegar bottles appear too large to carry. The larger drawing room is simply furnished, with a pair of eighteenth-century painted French chairs retaining their original needlework upholstery and a simple ochre-colored slab of *scagliola*, placed on metal gate finials to make an impressive center table.

On the floor above is the first of several terraces as well as the master bedroom suite. Rare Chinese antiques furnish the bedroom and glazed, earthenware pots of citrus decorate the terrace. The stone stairs narrow and wind around a stone column leading to a further floor, where the atmosphere changes from dimly lit patrician rooms to a broad, multi-level terrace, its plastered walls washed in rich pink, overlooking St Trophime Cathedral. It is difficult to discern when the rooms on this level were formed. On the street side is a single large room, now a guest suite, that may have been built in the late nineteenth century, but on the other side the stairs lead to two square rooms containing a wall of windows overlooking the Roman theater and the ancient roofs beyond. A bird's-eye view across the town and a reminder of the great height of the house is clear, as the central courtyard seems to be in complete darkness way below.

While grand and often highly detailed facades, crafted by master masons, announced community standing and social prestige, the interiors of the numerous Arles, Avignon and Aix-en-Provence town houses of the seventeenth and eighteenth centuries were restrained. Fireplaces provided the main statement in reception rooms but a quiet, restrained simplicity about the rooms and staircases has provided numerous generations with a fairly blank canvas for interior decoration. Dressed stone and plastered walls were more common than the elaborate *boiserie* of the cities. Paris fashion was not quick to come to the south and the splendor of Versailles had little impact in the provinces.

Massive wooden doors decorated with beaten metalwork and a gigantic lock open to the entrance lobby of a former monastic dwelling in Arles. Tiled floors lead to the original ground-floor salon and enclosed courtyard beyond. Close-set ceiling beams retain their early painted decoration in the main reception rooms.

ABOVE

Shallow-tread limestone stairs, worn by centuries of use, lead to the reception rooms on the first floor. Unadorned stone walls and a simple metal handrail enhance the monastic air, as does a small stained-glass window on a half-landing.

Reached from a secondary staircase and the salon, the kitchen is filled with over-scaled pieces collected from all over the world. The tabletop is part of an old painted ceiling, a cherry and elmwood draper's table from Lyon fills one wall, and wooden Spanish window trellis adds depth to the blank walls behind the kitchen counter.

KISMET

ABOVE & RIGHT

The collection of enormous amber and green glass vinegar bottles are from Trinquetaille, across the Rhône. Old silver and antique china form an effective still life on the draper's table. The painted center table is used for lunch every day but, when not in use, displays a changing hoard of favorite objects, collected mostly in France. The enormous Provençal wood and tole candlestick is used throughout the house, the pheasant hanging below a painting was found in Alsace, and fresh herbs, flowers and fruit are abundant in this much-used kitchen.

ABOVE & RIGHT

The tall hundred-year-old shutters on the petite salon windows have been left unpainted. The room forms the third side of the house around a deep courtyard below, and is furnished with just a pair of gilt French sofas and an intricately carved and painted bookcase.

ABOVE & OPPOSITE

A fine eighteenth-century stone fireplace featuring a central carved shell motif, the symbol of Arles, dominates the first-floor salon. Two pairs of metal gate finials form ideal legs, supporting a heavy scagliola tabletop upon which is part of a collection of Ming tomb guardians.

OPPOSITE & ABOVE

Antique Chinese priests' chairs, Japanese Imari and a seventeenth-century K'angshi vase, as well as a signed Ming bronze gong, all decorate the master bedroom. A rare old Mongolian tent lining hanging behind the bed is covered in a Thai silk bedcover from Jim Thompson.

ABOVE & OPPOSITE

The view from the uppermost terrace to another terrace off the main bedroom reveals

the complex jumble of rooflines and walls connecting adjacent buildings. Throughout

the summer, numerous antique Anduze pots are filled with geraniums.

LEFT & RIGHT

Beautifully formed arches and narrow passages leading off the ground-floor courtyard indicate how the house might have linked to its neighbors in the past. In deep shadow, with three floors rising above it, this is a cool and private retreat during the hottest days of summer.

BELOW RIGHT

The stone staircase narrows as it ascends to the top of the house, giving far-reaching views over St Trophime Cathedral and the Roman theater.

Lubéron

RUE DU MAUPAS

The ancient region between Cavaillon and Manosque contains some of the most beautiful villages in Provence, but the mellow stone houses and churches so tightly clustered on rocky hilltops and promontories belie their tumultuous past. Saracen invasions left the Montagne du Lubéron in a state of near ruin, but during the tenth century people began to group together and settle in the tight-knit communities that formed the nucleus of the protected villages we see today. Up until the early 1900s, numerous fortifications, now mostly demolished or collapsed, were still visible. Defence continued to play a part in village life up until World War II, when active centers of resistance were bombed. Strangely ignored by early geographers, the Via Domitia runs through it - the Parc du Lubéron still forms a compact world of its own, even though tourism now plays a significant part in the economy.

Restoration of medieval and Renaissance houses and castles is almost complete; such is the desire to experience life among the warren of narrow streets, ancient walls and turrets that have survived. It is an altogether different experience to that of life in a farmhouse on the plains below. The streets are narrow and access to many houses has not changed in centuries - no road-widening or so-called improvements have been enforced here. One asks for directions by name, not number, and it is likely that a simple wooden door set into a blank stone wall is the only evidence of life behind the towering, pale facades. Artists and writers were the vanguard of renewal after the war, with a stream of illustrious names taking up residence in villages such as Menerbes, Lacoste, Bonnieux and (especially) Gordes.

There is always a frisson when entering an enclosed space or opening a door to the unknown. This old village house was built in 1659. Though hardly wider than a large staircase, it was constructed with a stable at ground level, which until recently still had a compacted-earth floor. Slightly further up the narrow alley is the entrance to the house, which is reached via an outside stone staircase to the floor above. The structure is barely changed, although the stable has now become a study and the tiny entrance courtyard has been rejuvenated by the addition of an old basin, into which water trickles throughout the summer. River pebbles set into concrete and a pair of yellow-stemmed bamboo create a simple, calm and private space.

A hefty medieval stone gateway leads not to the village but just a storeroom, as it is blocked up with rubble stone and gives on to a blank wall. The somewhat precarious-looking stone steps have no railing and provide the only access into a sitting room on the right, whereas a bedroom and nautically inspired bathroom sit to their left. A portion of a wide, low arch across the rear of the sitting room indicates that the outer walls may have changed at some point, and also suggests that the next-door neighbors probably have the remainder of this arch jutting into their room. Layers of crumbling plaster were removed from the walls, so exposing the pale, almost white, limestone of the original structure.

These rooms had been used as a workshop for carding wool to make mattresses, and were in a pretty sorry state. New limestone block floors were laid down and a glass door was inserted into the outer wall. This door is the only light source on this level of the house, apart from the tiny windows in both the bedroom and bathroom.

A narrow stone staircase clings to the wall. This suggests that an even darker space will be found above; instead, the house opens up to a light-filled room with a glass door on to a street. A second sitting room, the kitchen and a further bedroom are housed on this level, with a timber staircase leading to a mezzanine and roof terrace above. It soon becomes clear just how steep these villages really are, as each level of the house is cut into the rocky cliff face below. A few meters along the street (or, rather, path), several layers of tiled roofs drop away to an even lower level. No doubt an architectural sleuth would be able to make sense of the myriad changes and evolution of these ancient dwellings, but time and again one finds blocked-up doorways, windows and changes of level within a single building.

The interior of this house has been developed with both summer and winter living firmly in mind. A capacious fireplace, a comfortable sofa and a wall of books together indicate an intimate cold-weather retreat, while bright colors and more windows in the room above naturally lead to the top of the house and the terrace overlooking rolling wooded hills (a valuable asset, as planning does not allow for the creation of new terraces). A charming country-style kitchen has been

This is typical of a stone-lined alley entrance to a house within one of the region's ancient walled towns. Built on steep-sided and rocky hills, the many street levels are linked by these preserved accessways.

built on the middle level in a room that previously contained no window, but rather than install a conventional framed window a large sheet of glass simply replaces the upper section of one wall. In a house that initially appears to resemble a large, hollow column, this is making the best use of space - at its widest and lightest point. Furnishings have been acquired on the basis of comfort, color and whimsy, while lighting has been organized to resemble Christmas decorations - tiny bulbs are draped and hung over furniture and along walls, and can be moved according to one's mood.

No architect sat down and drew up elaborate plans for this house or the dwellings surrounding it. However, if old houses are to be adapted to be suitable for continuous human habitation, clearly all it requires is the judicious use of the correct materials and a sensitivity to one's site and surroundings.

ABOVE RIGHT

The new staircase leading to the mezzanine and roof terrace can just be seen from the kitchen. Furniture is rustic and practical and, by choice, is all handmade by local craftsmen. Colors have been chosen to reflect light but without any fuss about matching one another too closely.

OPPOSITE & ABOVE LEFT

A new kitchen in an older style was created in the center of the house, lit by removing a section of the outer wall and replacing it with glass. Every effort has been made to use traditional local materials – the custom-made stone sink, the wall tiles, cupboards and carved chandelier all came from nearby villages.

LEFT

A former workshop is now the winter sitting room. Stripped of crumbling plaster, the walls are left in their original state, although the low arch at the end of the room indicates that at one time this was a much larger space. Prototype zebra chairs and a checkered rug from Paris add a whimsical note.

OPPOSITE

A new staircase and mezzanine were added to the salon, providing easy access to the roof terrace. Planning restrictions no longer allow terraces to be built on the old rooftop areas so, no matter how small, they are a greatly valued space in village houses.

ABOVE

Although a long way from the sea, the nautical bathroom is original and well made. Even the floors are a faithful replica of teak ships decking. This bathroom and the bedroom (opposite) are tucked into a space to the left of the entrance but maintain a sense of privacy, as the only other room in this area is the winter sitting room, at an unseen angle.

LEFT

The guest room features a tiny window and an eighteenth-century fireplace, a simple painted bed and cotton quilt. Heating is often difficult in very small rooms, but here the tall upright radiator in an alcove is perfect. To the right of the painted chest is a curtained storage area cut into the thick walls.

LEFT & ABOVE

At the end of an alleyway, a door opens on to the tiny, pebbled entrance courtyard. Behind the fruit picker's ladder is one of the original gateways into the old town and, just beyond the elegant fountain, a set of stone steps leads to the front door.

OPPOSITE

High above ground level is the small terrace with far-reaching views over the forest and the outer ring of village houses to the left and right.

THE MANOR HOUSE

Aix-en-Provence

PAVILLON DE VICTOIRE

Built in the late eighteenth century by the Archbishop of Avignon, the Pavillon de Victoire near Aix-en-Provence was originally a hunting lodge. The perfect pale-stone symmetrical facade is breathtaking, all the more so when the remarkable story of the house unfolds. Originally situated in Carpentras, nearly 130km (80 miles) away from its present site, the building was a ruin, but with immense foresight it was decided to move it stone by stone to a flat farm field with nothing to recommend it except an old oak *allée* and the solitude of a private agricultural estate.

Important elements such as the beautifully crafted stone staircase and the floor tiles were saved, as well as its cornerstones and other classical details. Although enlarged by the addition of a wing on either side of the original central block to accommodate an enormous kitchen and second living room, it is difficult to tell whether or not these single-storied wings are original; indeed, visitors assume the house has always been this way.

The approach is along an old, quiet and heavily wooded farm road. A pair of grand iron gates signals the expectation of a house, but one is not prepared for the restrained classical beauty of the pavilion as it comes into view along a line of severely clipped yew cones. Either side of the entrance there are rectangular fields - mown, but not manicured grass - leading the eye through old oaks to grazing horses, geese and hens. A line of antique Anduze pots and a pair of terracotta statues herald the main entrance. Unadorned apart from a pair of busts on plinths and pots containing bonsai-clipped holly, the wide gravel front is enclosed by barn-like structures (housing working studios) on either side. There is still no sign of the complex geometry and originality of the garden that is to come.

By adhering strictly to exterior and interior symmetry, a balance of uniformity and variety and, above all, livability, mid- to late eighteenth-century architecture reached a zenith of purity. Architects of the day had domesticated the "classic", and the last quarter

of the century witnessed a revival of interest in the country and countryside pursuits, along with the writings of Jean-Jacques Rousseau (that sophisticated advocate of the simple life), who had seized hold of the French imagination. So again, in the late twentieth century, a building that was about to disappear was recreated as a 1780s country house. Today we admire the chaste severity of the exterior and are both charmed and entranced by the innate delicacy of the interiors. The garden follows suit: fine, white river-gravel drives extend from the front along the sides of the house, and disappear into long vistas that terminate with massive wooden gates set into a high stone wall. In the top corners of the rectangle there are two east and west guest pavilions – perfect little houses in their own right – and between these and the main house the symmetrical grids that form the myriad garden "rooms" are laid out. Designed to stimulate at both ground level and from above, the garden looks exactly like its beautifully drawn and hand-colored

LEFT

Clipped holly and a pair of stone busts ornament an otherwise restrained and classical eighteenth-century country house. The central door opens into a stone-flagged staircase hall, with reception rooms to the left and the right. Set away from the house at right angles, a pair of barns balance – and slightly enclose – the entrance front.

original plan, thanks to the planting of a multitude of hedges, plus the layering of trees and clipping of olives into drum shapes.

Double wooden doors open on to the central hall, with an ancient stone staircase set foursquare in the middle of the house. All the small-paned windows are tall and narrow, perfectly in proportion to the size of the rooms, each of which is protected by full-height, painted shutters. The interiors are a peerless evocation of eighteenth-century *art de vivre*. An important collection of *boiserie* (paintings, furniture and carpets belonging to a family member), a fortunate discovery, sets the scene for the interior decoration in the style of the *ancien régime*. The main living rooms sit to the left and right of the hall, and a formal dining room lined with French chinoiserie panels is painted predominantly in pale yellow, enlivened by painted chairs and a table decorated with Masonic symbols.

An old-fashioned, fabric-lined door leads to a china and silver storage area, and beyond is the capacious kitchen, which runs along the full depth of the house. Eighteenth-century kitchens may have been essentially the dark, functional quarters of cooks and cleaners, but today the kitchen has also taken on the role of living room, and nevertheless has a great sense and atmosphere of times long past. Enormous old stone sinks have been positioned at either end, and in between there are runs of cupboards. One wall is

ABOVE & RIGHT

Both the entrance front shown here and the expansive formal gardens behind feature large antique pots, stone and terracotta sphinxes and busts, statues, vases and topiary birds and animals.

made up of tall reclaimed Provençal doors, opposite which there are painted and fabric-lined storage areas. All the mod cons are here, but they are barely noticeable. Lace at the windows, old blue-and-white floor and wall tiles, country furniture and a collection of animal paintings combine to create the quintessential rural haven, enhanced by bottles of home-made preserves and built-in dog beds.

On the opposite side of the hall is the formal salon, rich in texture, color and intrigue. A large but intimate space filled with portraits and magical landscapes, this room invites close encounters and old-fashioned formality - quite the opposite to the new sitting room beyond. Here full-height, oval-topped windows flood the room with light. Distressed woodwork on doors and bookshelves in shades of off-white blends with the hundreds of meters of beige-and-red-striped Belgian linen, which has been used to line the walls, upholster furniture and curtain the room. This is a summer living space: relaxed, casual and in direct contact with the south-facing seating area beyond, it is here that one can best contemplate the Provençal allure.

Essentially four rooms on top of four, the first floor (echoing the ground level) houses bedrooms and bathrooms decorated in the timeless, grand French style. Fabrics are from the old French textile houses, handmade carpets are laid on old terracotta tiles, furniture is Provençal or Parisian, and books abound. Each of the three bedrooms has a marble bathroom; the fourth room is used as a study. Celadon-green walls are lined with a collection of monotone, red chalk drawings of the house and its garden, all framed identically. Throughout, the furniture and decoration has the same intensity, a cohesive weight and depth of color, texture and quality. Pavillon de Victoire is the embodiment of all that French rural life promises: the grand and the informal, and a house and garden that stimulate all our senses but, equally, allow repose.

LEFT

The formal dining room is lined with French chinoiserie panels that had languished in storage for decades. Italian painted and caned chairs surround a Louis XVII-style table decorated with painted Masonic symbols, and through the old-fashioned fabric-lined door is the large farmhouse kitchen.

OPPOSITE

Heavy stone door-frames link the dining room and grand salon to the entrance hall. Set further back in the hall is a superb original stone staircase that leads to the first floor.

Provence is justifiably famous for its craftsmen, who produce all manner of practical and beautifully made everyday items. As stone was, and still is, plentiful, kitchen sinks were made in numerous shapes and sizes, and unlike granite is soft to the touch. Although this example is very old, local craft is encouraged in the most positive way. People buy locally from family firms who have a long tradition of artisanal skill. In France, quality and durability are highly prized.

ABOVE & OPPOSITE

The kitchen is housed in one of two new symmetrical wings, which have been added to the original house. Walls of antique cupboards are filled with china, while (opposite) fabric-lined cupboards hold glassware and hide fridges. A pair of heavy, very old stone sinks are set into the work counters at either end of the room, and so large is the space that a sixteen-seat table sits easily between.

LEFT & ABOVE

Inspired by Moroccan interiors, and using vast of amounts of Belgian striped linen, the summer sitting room opens on to a walled, private garden through oval-topped double doors. The large polo painting and several other works are by renowned animal painter Aurélien Raynaud.

OPPOSITE

Bracquénie fabric is used on the walls and for curtains in this guest bedroom, in classic French style. One of a collection of oriental carpets adorns the tiled floor and an important gilt mirror hangs between a pair of tall, narrow windows. All the furniture is Provençal.

RIGHT

Three bedroom suites and an enchanting study fill the first floor. Each of the en-suite bathrooms features fine marble and generous use of "document" French cotton fabrics.

Elegant iron gates open on to an enclosed gravel terrace immediately behind the house, which in turn leads through to the first of the formal garden "rooms". In each top corner of the formal garden stands a miniature pavillon, *perfectly scaled and comprising a complete house set in an individual private garden. The formal garden seen from the staircase-landing window (opposite) demonstrates the elegant geometry applied to the numerous "rooms" and enclosures through careful planting.*

A spring-fed pond at the rear of the garden is watched over by a
Florentine wild boar fountain (above right). A pair of dramatic, red
Anglo-Chinese benches (opposite) provides a shock of color and surprise
in this largely green and white garden. Most Provençal houses have a bell
to announce one's arrival at the side door (above left). Throughout the
garden there are myriad fountains and ponds.

LES MAS DU GRÈS

Local farmers remember when Les Mas du Grès was a small, simple farmhouse that served as both café and local meeting place. Built in about 1820, the original two-storied rectangular house remained at the core of an extensive building programme to enlarge and balance the house, creating open, flowing spaces with easy access, and good views across the intricately formal garden on one side and a broad, sheltered terrace on the other.

Provençal winters can be harsh and cold, and its summers blindingly hot, so the planning focused on good light and air-flow as well as providing intimate and sheltered spaces for reading, watching films, listening to music and indoor entertaining. Taking architectural tradition into account and echoing an existing structure on the property, the owners decided to raise both ends of the house above the original roofline. Built of rough stone and plastered, only the plainest Provençal detail prevails: slim stone door and window cases and some exposed cornerstones are the only relief against the pale-yellow exterior walls. From the inside, however, the changing light levels and the enormously tall staircase window provide quite a different sense of the architecture to that which is seen from the outside. At no point can one see the entire house from the garden - old plane trees shadow the facade from an entrance at the furthest point of the lawn and topiary garden, while a pair of solid gates allows access on one side, enabling just a glimpse of the kitchen wing and terrace above. Even the broad front terrace is swathed in green. An ancient fig tree, its branches resting like tentacles on the ground, breaks up the well-proportioned windows and doors, all of which are shuttered and painted an old, dull white.

The entire ground floor has been laid with reclaimed, eighteenth-century Burgundy limestone flags, ranging in color from cream and pink to grey and almost green, and in random sizes and finishes. Some are polished to a brilliant sheen; others have a pitted surface, or are slightly uneven from centuries of wear and tear. These floors are spectacular in themselves and, with only the minimum of carefully chosen furniture in each room, provide a strong design feature. Unusually, the main entrance is off-center, marked by an ancient oak door with a simple ironwork latch.

To the right is a supremely elegant, new stone staircase rising through the double height of the tower-like extension. A specialist ironworker from Burgundy made the beautifully crafted handrail after a design found in an eighteenth-century synagogue nearby, and a pair of old Provençal doors hides cloakroom and storage areas under the stairs.

A line of interlinking rooms progresses from the hall to the kitchen, but there is no corridor to block out light or shut away the gently defined spaces. First there is the petite salon, part-library and winter dining room, followed by the formal (though summery) dining room, and the kitchen, in the oldest part of the house. Spanning the full width of the house, it contains the most important original element of the old *mas*, its enormous stone fireplace. The only source of heat until late in the twentieth century, it was here that the life of the farmhouse took place and to some extent still does. The table, specially designed for the kitchen, is made of French oak with three black slate inserts on the top, and heavy oak legs painted to resemble the slate above. It is here, surrounded by a collection of

American Arts and Crafts chairs, that fourteen people regularly sit down to meals in the winter. Above the dogs' beds beside the fire are a worktop and walls covered in handmade tiles from Apt, an old tile-making center that still produces traditional tiles of all colors.

What might be called a secondary hall runs across the garden front of the house and contains a new oak stairway leading to the first floor. Instead of stone or tile, the floors have been laid with oak boards, and sanded down but not sealed. From the main stone stairway, the top floor opens out into what appears to be a large empty space with only a *radassière*, a Turkish-inspired day bed covered with a handmade, Central European quilt and Venetian velvet cushions. The room is designed for watching films on a large, drop-down screen, but all the technical gear has been subtly hidden behind a wall of oak cupboards. The ceilings become lower as guest quarters emerge in the old structure (with its small, almost attic-sized windows), but once again at the opposite end of the floor - in counterbalance to the stairwell - the main bedroom suite reveals towering beamed ceilings with tall windows and doors leading to a private, west-facing terrace with its own fountain. The bathrooms are modern marvels of fine marble and chrome.

As the property is surrounded by tall, clipped hedges and has no rural outlook, the design of the garden became as architecturally refined as the house.

An ochre-washed wall links the house to a garden room, creating a private seating area before opening on to a wide border in the formal garden. Numerous white gravel paths divide the garden into individual blocks of color and pattern.

The rectangular-shaped formal planting is of staggering exactitude. Thousands of box plants were laid out, not to form a hedge but to be clipped into individual drums, defining innumerable enclosures for the display of vivid summer bedding. Clashing dahlias, petunia, cosmos daisies and verbena shimmer in the sunlight. Fine gravel paths intersect numerous axes and clipped cypress tower like exclamation marks at key points. Beyond the Persian carpet of color, and on the slightest downward slope, lies the water garden set within an old pine woodland. Three diminishing-sized, stone-edged pools finish at the "water temple", an eighteenth-century stone bell tower (one of a pair) that was originally situated atop a key building in Marseille.

Though much restored and enlarged, Les Mas du Grès is undoubtedly Provençal. Its proportions and materials are correct, according to the way the natural evolution and development of these old houses would have progressed. The fireplaces, floors, windows, doors, terraces, tiles and garden all look right - testament to the "improving" owners of Provençal heritage.

OPPOSITE & ABOVE LEFT

A view from the main entrance doors over the raised topiary garden (opposite). The terrace fills the entire width of the house, providing several seating areas opening off the kitchen. Beyond the plane trees is an enclosed swimming pool surrounded by trees and lined with flowerpots. The delightful old brass drop (above) is used as a door knocker.

ABOVE RIGHT

Reclaimed seventeenth-century oak doors lead into the capacious, flagstoned entrance hall. On the right is the new staircase showing part of the double-height windows that light the hall. Apart from a pair of tall cupboards and a cast-iron urn, the space has been deliberately left empty, allowing an uninterrupted view through the salon to the formal garden beyond.

LEFT

Fine eighteenth-century Burgundy flagstone floors provide the perfect foundation for a collection of superb, mostly antique furniture, including this pair of Louis XVII chairs from a chateau nearby. The modern oak staircase leads to the master suite.

OPPOSITE

The main entrance is flooded with light from the new staircase window. Looking to the left, one can see through the petite salon, the dining room, and beyond to the kitchen at the opposite end of the house.

ABOVE

*Terriers sleep in specially made houses under the handmade tiled worktop, with
a shelf displaying a fine collection of early copperware and lead planters below.
The door on the right leads to the utility rooms.*

LEFT

*With a low ceiling and original, gigantic stone fireplace, this was the heart of the
old house. French oak and volcanic slate were used to make the table, while the
chairs are 1920s American Arts and Crafts.*

ABOVE

Used for reading and occasional dining, the contemporary Italian hexagonal table was made from old ebony and walnut parquet flooring, bound together with a cast-iron trim. Rose Tarlow at Melrose House supplied the original candlestick, and a group of Regency-style chairs are upholstered in striped horsehair.

RIGHT

Several sets of French doors, hung with a double-layer of fine Belgian linen, lead from the salon to the broad front terrace. The console table and pair of French fauteuils with needlework upholstery are eighteenth-century.

91

LES MAS DU GRÈS

LEFT & OPPOSITE

The magnificent new Le Baux stone staircase rises through two floors in a specially extended wing on the east side of the house. Reclaimed Provençal doors on either side lead to cloakrooms, and the masterly ironwork railings were an adaptation of an eighteenth-century design found in a Provence synagogue.

ABOVE & RIGHT

Old oak planks, sanded but not sealed, cover the first floor. A magnificent open-plan room at the top of the staircase is lined with oak cupboards containing a sophisticated home cinema, viewed from a radassière, a Turkish daybed draped with an Eastern European velvet patchwork quilt and Venetian velvet cushions.

OPPOSITE

A Louis XIII fireplace is the focal point in the master bedroom. A pair of doors lead on to a private terrace that, even on the first floor, has an old stone fountain set on one wall. The red cashmere bed cover has a richly embroidered centerpiece, and an Italian fortuny silk light appears to float below the immensely high, beamed ceiling.

ABOVE & OPPOSITE

The cloakroom basin (above), a seventeenth-century design, was made from a local orange marble, and the new taps are copies of those commonly found in Aix-en-Provence. Sarragon marble from the Pyrenees has been used extensively in the master bath and shower room (opposite). Indeed, all the bathrooms in the house feature different-colored marbles of superb quality, plus deep baths and views over the formal garden.

OPPOSITE

On the topiary terrace, quirky shapes are silhouetted against the pale facade and create convivial seating areas. Modern teak furniture is weathering to a silver-grey color in the sun, but at the kitchen end a traditional metal frame is covered in vines and creepers, providing summer shade.

ABOVE LEFT & RIGHT

Beyond and slightly below the formal garden, and shaded by a pine grove, is the contemplative water garden (right), punctuated by an eighteenth-century stone bell tower from Marseille. At one time every house had its own well close to the kitchen (left), and most of them, like this one, have been retained although are not in use. An ancient fig has bent so much that the terrace now supports its main branches.

LEFT & RIGHT

Seen from a bedroom balcony, the formal garden
is reminiscent of a vivid Persian carpet.
Hundreds of clipped box drums edge beds of
clashing summer colors comprised of petunias,
dahlias, cosmos daisies and verbena. Columns of
cypress line the central path, whereas the outer
borders contain shrubs and numerous roses.

Carnoules

DOMAINE DU GRAND CROS

When the Paris Assembly decreed in 1790 that France should be divided into 83 equal squares, the Var *département* was the first of three (along with Bouches-de-Rhône and Basses-Alpes) to be created in Provence. Fortunately the squares changed to take into account local customs, language and tradition - Vaucluse was added in 1793 when papal ownership was given up, then (in 1860) the Alpes-Maritimes in 1860. Officially the region of Provence had disappeared by total absorption into France: empty of population compared to the Vaucluse, it is the coastal towns and cities of the Var that are best known: Toulon, the home to the French Navy; Hyères, the oldest of the southern French winter resorts; plus St Tropez and Roman Fréjus. The sparsely populated valleys of the Issole and Argens rivers, east of the Durance, were highly productive in Greek and Roman times and, although not highlighted in many of the major Provençal tourist guides, apart from noting bauxite production in Brignoles, the region thrives as the center of Côte de Provence wine production, an *appellation contrôlée* that is almost exclusive to the Var.

Domaine du Grand Cros, in the village of Besse-sur-Issole, comprises 22 hectares (54 acres) of vines, dry-stone terraces, a new olive plantation, a modern winery and a large house, but years ago things were quite different. Once part of a much larger estate, and certainly noted in local records from the 1700s, the property had been abandoned for another establishment for over twenty-five years, although some of the previous owners' pets continued to inhabit the house. The oldest section was built on a very large rock, hence the name of Grand Cros, derived from an old Provençal word meaning "eye of the tooth". Choosing a solid foundation explains why the back of the house is a good deal higher than the front and why the sweeping front terrace is 2m (6ft) above ground level. The property is surrounded by forest now, but there are ancient wild olive groves within it and numerous remains of the Roman aqueducts that carried water great distances. The longest in France was the coastal 50km (30 mile) Mons to Fréjus stretch.

When the present family bought the property, the house and winery were merged. The terrace contained a laundry and chicken house, and the master bedroom was home to the water collection tank that ran down a pipe into the drawing room (formerly the kitchen). There was no plumbing in the rest of the house, the current kitchen was a stable and the roof had partially collapsed. Work began immediately to release the full potential of the *terroir* (soil) - old rootstock was removed and a new programme of planting undertaken, using modern methods for organic production. In 2002, after years of sustained hard work and research, a rose from this estate was chosen to accompany the Queen's Golden Jubilee dinner.

A great deal of rationalization had to be carried out in the house. Typically, the north side had no windows, and by adding a few the floor levels had to be altered. On the ground floor it was discovered that the floor tiles were laid on to the bedrock, so when new limestone blocks were brought in they were set on a bed of sand with heating beneath. To balance the imposing facade, a new three-storied wing was added to the central projecting bay, and French doors added along the whole front, allowing access from the reception rooms to the terrace.

The winery (*cave*), still attached to the house, now forms a courtyard at the rear. Built on several levels, with new retaining walls and steps, it is now the best way to move between the two. Visitors enter the house through a large, dramatic hall, at the building's rear, where the old outer walls have been partly removed. Some of the many old bedrooms have been converted into bathrooms and dressing rooms and, though now reduced in number, the suites are enviably large and light. The front of the house is washed in a faded pink and the rear in a soft yellow ochre. Its shutters match the grey-white cornerstones of the building.

In summer the vast front terrace is completely shaded by several 200-year-old plane trees and, as home and business are closely intertwined, this terrace is used constantly for wine tastings, lunches, meetings and sales. In fact, so busy is the summer season that a chef is employed to cater for friends, colleagues and customers. A charming cottage set a few steps off the terrace has been restored as a guesthouse but, while work was being carried out, some very early, carved stone feeding troughs (probably for pigs) were discovered. These troughs are a rare curiosity, however, so have been left in place. Planting around the house is limited to mostly pots, although a 12 sq m (130 sq ft) rose garden has been added to break up the expanse of front lawn; a forest of bamboo that was encroaching on the house was removed early on.

The layout of the ground floor now makes total sense. The kitchen is situated at one end and leads to the formal dining room, the only room where color has been employed – an old-fashioned terracotta wall finish that glows in candlelight. The capacious drawing room, with two separate seating areas, is pale and sophisticated, furnished with objects collected during the owners' travels. A Normandy commode and English Hepplewhite chairs were bought in Canada, the sofas were found in Geneva, the rugs in India, and the dining-room table came from Ireland. The silky texture of old white- and woad-dyed linen sheets make them ideal for bedroom curtains, either clipped to metal poles or draped over wooden poles with finials.

Domaine du Grand Cros was brought back from the brink in more ways than one. The property illustrates nicely the constant renewal and commitment that Provençal residents bring to the countryside around them.

RIGHT

Complementary natural pigments have been used on the exterior walls. Over time the colors mottle and fade and improve with age, unlike modern paintwork, which relies on a pristine, clean finish to impress. The beautifully laid tile roofs provide strong structural lines against the plain walls.

ABOVE

The main entrance leads in all directions with rooms forming an enclosed courtyard linking the cave (winery) to the house. An office and library are set into one corner, straight ahead is the olive planted patio and to the left – down several steps – is the entrance hall, to the right.

OPPOSITE

Old doors are reused in the newly built entrance hall, which links the study and courtyard buildings to the main house. Exterior walls have been cut away at various points along the north side, creating a more formal entry point that was previously confined to the front terrace. A collection of Ming and Tang jars were bought in Kerala, India, and the Provençal fruitwood armoire was found locally.

ABOVE

Here, the inner hall gives us a glimpse into the warmly colored formal dining room (the only room where warm colors have been employed). Wide and well lit from both sides, the new hall allows free access from one end of the house to the other.

OPPOSITE

The original staircase and railings survived the building works, but the hall layout has been changed and improved. Double doors from the dining room allow plenty of light through to the hall that leads to both the kitchen and drawing room. Botanical prints line the walls and tapestry-covered hall chairs stand opposite.

ABOVE

A marble-topped café table serves as a drinks table in the kitchen. Copious limed-oak cupboards – as well as tall dressers and a large country table and chairs – fill the kitchen that links to both the front terrace and a secluded side-terrace facing the pool.

OPPOSITE

Rich terracotta-colored walls glow at night in the formal dining room. Thick silk curtains, a vivid oriental carpet and gilt mirrors decorate a room that is used for dinner parties in the winter. In between the pair of tall French doors is a pretty, carved nineteenth-century stone fireplace.

ABOVE & OPPOSITE

A wall of French doors allows the double drawing room to extend on to the main terrace in summer. Books spill out of the library,
bouquets of flowers abound, and plenty of generous sofas provide seating for large numbers of people. The colorful picture above
the patterned sofa is by Sylvia Brauerman, bought from the artist in Vence. The dining room can be seen through double doors
at the end of the room.

ABOVE & OPPOSITE

Beautifully made ironwork screens and window latches are typical of old Provençal houses. The master bedroom was formerly where the water tanks were housed, but a major redesign of the first-floor rooms created several bedroom and bathroom suites from a warren of smaller rooms. The iron bed was bought in Paris.

An old run-down cottage has been restored for guests but centuries-old, rare, carved-stone feeding troughs were found underneath. Vines surround the house on all sides, with forest beyond. The garden clings close to the cottage but plans to develop the gardens further are well under way.

THE COUNTRY HOUSE

Lacoste

LES MACCANS

Described as dark, dank, uncompromisingly challenging and a home only to rabbits, this old farmhouse sat forlornly in 3 hectares (7 acres) of aged vines, long grass and a couple of cherry trees - even the vines had to be ripped out when the property was acquired as part of a government scheme to reduce grape production. The story of its rehabilitation and that of other local projects has been recounted in a delightful book, *The Lubéron Garden*, written by the owner. A typical rural construction of thick rubble-stone walls, clay-tiled roof and blank north face, it nestles in a gently folding landscape, moulded and contoured by centuries of agriculture and, more recently, a little intervention by a man on a mission. In the 1960s, "improvements" had been carried out, including the addition of hollow wooden doors, replacement windows and wood-chip wallpaper, all of which had to be removed. Most of the old roof tiles were intact, although the roof dipped precariously in the middle.

At first sight the house appears to be a simple rectangle - with two floors and level terraces on every side - but the interior layout belies the plain, rural facade. The south side of the ground floor had disappeared beneath a bank of earth and the "garden" threatened to engulf the rest, and before work could begin on the house a great deal of earth-moving was carried out to push the encroaching land away from the property. The largest windows face west but the gable ends are aligned roughly north-south and, as there is no obvious main entrance, it was decided to level out seating areas on all four sides and to create grassy terraces that curve and roll rather than the more usual straight-edged, agricultural variety.

Although set well below the village of Lacoste and its massive castle (once owned by the notorious Marquis de Sade), the views over the intensely cultivated farmland are broad and spectacular, rimmed by the solid and inert Lubéron mountain range in the distance.

Unlike those farmsteads set foursquare in the plains, every window in this house frames a different scene, rather like those fold-out postcards entitled "Scenes from Provence". There is a river of lavender running down the hill into what is called the wine lake - a pond with a small group of vines above it. Climbing roses, lavender and perovskia, olive, almond and quince are but a handful of the large variety of plants chosen for their hardiness, beauty and scent. While May is warm and sunny, and gardens are at their best, being able to understand plant performance in this unforgiving climate - where winter temperatures can drop to -15°C (5°F), and shoot up to 40°C (104°F) in July - is a key factor when establishing planting schemes that can survive this onslaught.

Work on the house began after the back-breaking job of landscaping was complete. The ground floor (which was part animal shelter and farm storage, and still had earth floors) was cleared out; new stone floors were laid; and several windows and doors were cut through the thick stone walls. Where possible the old shutters were retained, many with blistered paint and rather unsteady on their hinges. Two pebble paths converge on a covered terrace outside the kitchen, which now houses an old wood- and zinc-topped bar and plenty of simple open shelving for storage. On one side of the kitchen narrow stone stairs lead up to the first floor and, beyond, through a plain arch, is the large square dining room with doors on to a terrace. The rest of the ground floor contains a large, light drawing room, with a further set of glass doors at one end and an enormous fireplace at the other. A hefty stone buttress projecting into the room and an old stone arch next to it would indicate that this part of the house, with a double-height ceiling, was added at a later date. Massive square beams running lengthwise through the kitchen and dining room support the floors above and, although the ceilings are low, the use of soft white paint throughout relieves any feeling of oppression. A mezzanine floor was built over half the drawing room to form a winter sitting room and library. Deep sofas, copious bookshelves, a writing table and large fireplace provide a draught-free bolthole in the coldest months.

There is a great lightness about the interiors, partly through the choice of simple country furniture, mostly painted off-white, and also because the rooms are not cluttered. Curtains in the drawing room are made of thickly gathered hessian sackcloth, and faded linen has been chosen for outdoor cushions and upholstery. An old Indian quilt has been used as a tablecloth, watering cans are displayed like sculpture and, above all, every part of the house is lived in and comfortable. Bedrooms and bathrooms on the first floor have tall windows and wooden floors, some covered with seagrass, others left polished and plain.

The main bedroom was probably the former living room, evidenced by the monolithic fireplace now painted white, and in a break from the all-white theme the walls have been rubbed with yellow ochre. Beds and baths are copious. Cotton quilts and curtains are light and pale, and fresh flowers are artlessly displayed all over the house in whatever container comes to hand. Set under a group of old oaks and in deep shade is a ubiquitous stone table and bench, but each terrace has a collection of rustic café chairs, metal day beds and weathered teak tables, providing summer diners with differing views of the garden and valley below. The stone-edged swimming pool sits unobtrusively in folding grass terraces and is backed by a beautifully built dry-stone wall, beyond which grow a profusion of roses punctuated by slender columns of clipped cypress.

Few people who dream of their own little patch in Provence would have the imagination or the fortitude to translate such bucolic romanticism into reality. However, skill combined with sheer hard work proves that dreams really can come true if only you want them to.

ABOVE LEFT & OPPOSITE

Entered from a sheltered covered terrace, the kitchen has plenty of generous, but simple open shelving, used for storage. Massive square beams run lengthwise through the kitchen and adjoining dining room. The wood and zinc bar counter is said to have been rescued from a fire in Lacoste's Café de France *fifty years ago.*

ABOVE RIGHT

Opening off the kitchen is the large square dining room. The choice of simple country furniture gives a lightness to the interior of the house – here, a simple painted dresser, table and chairs, painted in off-white. The sitting room, which is visible through the arch, was converted from an earth-floored barn and tractor shed.

Doors swathed in tobacco-colored hessian replace an old barn door in the double-height end of the sitting room, where decoration has been kept simple by the extensive use of white paint. An old court chair and several other chairs have been painted, upholstery is plain cotton and linen, and Moroccan straw mats add a touch of color. A section of an intricately carved wooden grille hangs above the fireplace.

ABOVE LEFT & ABOVE RIGHT

Old doors make an effective headboard in the master bedroom, which was probably the original living room. The large fireplace (above right) was added during the 1960s renovation. All the bedrooms and bathrooms have a country-house feel, where comfort is paramount.

OPPOSITE

The mezzanine floor – furnished with deep sofas, a fireplace and a wall of books – was rebuilt above the sitting room to form a winter library and sitting room, which proves to be an essential draught-free escape when temperatures drop to -15°C (5°F) in winter.

ABOVE & RIGHT

Climbing roses will soon form a tunnel on the approach to the north end of the house (above). Careful landscaping has ensured there are outdoor living areas off all the main rooms, and (right) old bed frames cut in half were originally used as day beds during the grape pickers' vendange (harvest). The choice of furniture ranges from teak benches and parasols to wrought-iron or painted-wood café chairs. Simple candle lanterns proliferate, linen-covered cushions are numerous, and each terrace has a completely different view of the garden and valley below.

ABOVE

A simple, stone-edged swimming pool has been set into a newly created terrace slightly above the level of the house. Sheltered and largely out of sight, it is surrounded by a profusion of roses and columns of clipped cypress.

OPPOSITE

In his book The Lubéron Garden, *the owner describes the complex business of gaining planning permission for this (now freestanding) gate. The river-pebble path leads to the shady kitchen terrace.*

MAS DU MANESCAU

St Rémy-de-Provence, birthplace of astrologist Nostradamus and gateway to the Alpilles, is probably the most well-known and best-loved town in western Provence. Firmly centered within the "golden triangle", its town houses, boulevards and squares, courtyards and alleyways epitomize a romantic past and slower pace of life. While the town and nearby Plateau des Antiques attract numerous visitors, it is the gentle countryside, so dramatically punctuated by the stark, majestic, eroded ridges of the Alpilles, that has drawn an international coterie of property collectors, who have led the way in the rehabilitation of innumerable old *mas* and *bastides*. The roads that radiate out from the town into the fertile agricultural lands, bisected by cascading irrigation canals, take one through a kaleidoscope of Provençal history from arguably France's most exquisite Roman arch and mausoleum to the priory of St Paul de Mausole, where Vincent van Gogh painted some of his more luminous pictures.

By their very nature secluded and unseen from the road, the most desirable country properties are to be found scattered throughout the old wheat and sheep farms of the old agricultural order. Today, market gardening, seed and fresh flower production has taken over, and magnificent gardens have replaced sheep pens and barns, but there is a palpable sense of a sustained attachment to the old pastoral life. Land remains a precious commodity to the *Provençaux* and, although many of the old farmhouses have been sold with a small amount of land, family smallholdings continue to flourish between well-spaced houses with grapes or flowers growing on every tiny parcel of land.

Mas du Manescau was formerly the village smithy (or forge), and nearby a similar stone-built dwelling of the same period housed the local beekeeper. Set on the edge of a small canal and facing the Alpilles, the house is hidden by hedges, plane trees and olives. Just a glimpse of the tiled roof and the tops of its white-painted shutters are visible from the

narrow track leading to the house. Stone gate piers and an old wooden gate lead to an expansive terrace that is enclosed, private, paved and shaded. The ancient well is home to a climbing rose and a stone fountain trickles into a basin. To the left are lavender beds set into symmetrical river-pebble enclosures, and beyond is a dark-hued pool anchored by sentinel cypress columns. The land is flat, but an area of rough grass is regularly clipped at differing heights before being allowed to run riot as a wild-flower meadow before disappearing into a group of soaring oaks and the forest beyond.

Apart from the outer walls and some of the windows, little remains of the original workshop and its scant living accommodation attached. The philosophy behind the extensive renovation was to create a contemporary home that was light all year. The owner, a distinguished interior designer and antiques dealer, wanted open spaces, flexible living areas and plenty of volume while keeping a Provençal feel. Walls came down and the ground floor was rationalized to create

LEFT

Limestone gate piers support an elegant, but weather-beaten pair of painted gates. The entrance to the house was moved away from the front of the house, allowing a view along the terrace over the original well to a fountain placed at right angles to the house. A red rose growing outside is the only splash of color in the largely silver, green and white

an open-plan living and dining room with an integral (although barely visible) kitchen in what had been the smithy. The large room has lofty beamed ceilings and leads to a winter conservatory that faces the garden, with a studio and library behind replacing what was a stable. An integral terrace extends from the studio into the garden, and under a traditional open-sided outbuilding there is a cool summer dining area with its own kitchen. Large, white limestone blocks replaced the old floors and plain, square arches link the ground-floor rooms. A more formal salon with a superb seventeenth-century fireplace is at the center of the house, forming the main entrance. To one side is a study, leading to a small internal hall from which the tile and timber staircase leads to the upper floor. Spacious utility rooms and a wine store complete the ground-floor design.

As only one half of the house is two-storied, the top floor is relatively small and has no warren of passages or hallways. Partway up the staircase, the wall has been replaced with a glass screen that allows light to penetrate deep into the stairwell. At the top, the floor divides almost equally into two large bedrooms, each with en-suite bathrooms, both of which appear to be carved from blocks of limestone. Milky-white paint continues from the ground floor to the upper level and is used for walls, ceilings, shutters, windows, doors and beams alike. White cotton duck

The single-storied addition has lofty ceilings and expansive living space that incorporates an open-plan kitchen and dining area. Decoration is limited to the natural tones of stone, wood and pale leather. An untitled artwork by Greg Renfrow hangs above the kitchen, while beyond the Conran dining table and chairs there is a painting, Elpida Georgiou's Boxer Shorts. *A pair of symmetrical arches leads at one end to the west-facing, conservatory-style breakfast room and, at the other end, to the main drawing room, which is furnished simply with antiques.*

upholstery, tailor-made bed covers and crisp linen add to the fresh, light-hearted feel of the house. The judicious mix of antique and contemporary furniture is displayed in the best tradition of sophisticated modern interiors. The bedrooms remain simple and uncluttered through carefully planned storage areas. A glamorous seventeenth-century Italian bed and side-tables dominate the guest room, while the large master bedroom has a plainer bed but a curvaceous, linen-covered chaise longue and antique chest of drawers. Drops of unlined, off-white linen serve as curtains.

Athough the house was two years in the making, both builder and decorator have achieved rare harmony in the flow of its indoor and outdoor spaces. New doors allow better access to all the terraces, rooms link to

one another in the correct places, and internal doors are few, allowing contact from room to room. Careful consideration was given not only to the materials used but also to the finishes. Polished or unpolished floors, the shape of the delicate plaster curve running off the bottom step of the stairs, paint finishes, textural changes in the hard surfaces - even the choice of plant containers reflects a careful study of unifying elements. Every centimeter of space has been used to best effect, most noticeably by the number of books lining the walls and the design eliminating all the complicated little rooms so beloved of generations past. Both the house and its garden are irretrievably linked by their complementary architectural strengths and an enviable simplicity.

RIGHT

Unglazed, early twentieth-century Pueblo Indian pots used for grain and flour storage were bought from a specialist dealer in San Francisco. Made of clay and colored with natural pigments, the low sheen was achieved by polishing each pot with a stone.

OPPOSITE

An eighteenth-century stone fire surround was bought in St Rémy. Although the house is centrally heated, fires are lit throughout the sometimes bitterly cold winters. Hanging on the wall above is a plaster, bas-relief frieze, probably used as a model for stonecarvers.

ABOVE & RIGHT

Like the kitchen, although the low ceilings indicate this is the oldest part of the house, the central drawing room features several sets of glass doors leading to the terrace. Contemporary chairs and a sofa facing the seventeenth-century fireplace are covered in white cotton. A pair of Spanish clay pots, their original use unknown, are treated as sculptures on either side of the fire. Above a granite-topped, English console table hangs L'Enchanteresse by E. Chabin. Works of art inject the only color into these milk-white interiors. The long-legged dalmatian is painted papier mâché.

OPPOSITE

Series Squares by Ida Kohlmayer dominates the back wall of the drawing room. A grand piano fills one corner of the room, while the walnut chaise longue is ideally placed for a private concert. The rug is a rare 1920s American Navajo Indian piece, and of superb quality.

ABOVE

A large painting above the bed faces another bucolic scene, Albert Hadjiganev's Côte Normande. The modern metal chaise longue was bought in Paris, the chest of drawers is eastern European, and the enormous bronze-framed mirror above it is late nineteenth-century French. The lamp base was originally bought as a piece of sculpture.

LEFT & BELOW

Both the first-floor bathrooms feature seamless limestone blocks used in a variety of ways. The guest basin is cut from a single piece of stone and both rooms contain large showers hidden behind free-standing walls. This form of severe simplicity requires the finest materials and superb finishing.

OPPOSITE

The original staircase, formerly enclosed by a door, is intact but greatly improved by the addition of three white limestone steps linking to an elegantly curved plaster detail flaring from the walls. Glimpsed beyond the painted chest of drawers and a Chester Arnold painting, Elegies 2, is the dual-aspect study furnished with a mix of rustic and sophisticated tables and chairs.

ABOVE & OPPOSITE

Linked to the house by a custom-made metal trellis smothered in wisteria, the curtained outdoor kitchen (above left) is used throughout the summer. Provençal houses usually have several shaded dining or reading areas, positioned to be cool in summer but bright throughout the winter. English teak chairs by Charles Verey (above right) have weathered to a deep silver grey. The ceramic tree trunk table is Victorian. The bedrooms have full-height windows overlooking a canopy of sculptural plane trees and the Alpilles beyond. Echoing the soft white interiors, the shutters, windows and doors have all been painted off-white (opposite).

LEFT & ABOVE

There is a blur of distinction between the conservatory and the garden. Pale limestone continues from the house on to the west-facing pool terrace, designed by Jim Stringer, and disappear into the wild-flower field beyond. Set against a densely wooded background is a gigantic aluminium sculpture – Anne Wendling's Vivant *(left). A climbing rose is trained over a metal frame above the old well on the terrace.*

LES BAS ARTÈMES

Even among the traffic-choked roads of Provence in summer, it only takes a detour of a few kilometers to discover hidden gems, perhaps strongholds of peace and quiet. Firmly anchored 200m (680ft) above an intensively farmed valley below, Les Bas Artèmes appears as a feudal manor: self-contained, self-sufficient, inward-looking and wrapped in forest apart from the south front. From certain angles the rooflines indicate an entire village or at least an *hameau* (hamlet), enhanced by the sight of an ancient trackway, a visible sign of the network of rural paths and roads linking the region's hilltop villages and lowland farms. It is easy to imagine heavily laden donkeys scrambling up and down the hills, watering at cold springs and resting under the scrubby oak and pine that thrive in these hills. Truffle hunters with their dogs sniff out and pluck their harvest in the winter; wild boar are seen regularly; pine marten, foxes, squirrels, badgers, vipers and hare coexist with people in their bustling, mechanized world.

There is nothing of the simple rectangular *mas* of the plains here. Hidden in the center of a courtyard, attached to a group of former farm buildings, is the oldest part of the house. A low-vaulted room as solid as a bomb shelter, this would have been the heart of the farm, where a precious flock of sheep was housed during the winter before summering on the hillsides. Numerous rooms link to this old structure, now a dining room, but frequent changes of angle and level indicate centuries of addition and growth. There is no obvious entrance, though one is drawn to the south by a network of paths and vistas leading to a series of terraces, the lowest of which houses a vast swimming pool. On the east side of the main house (forming part of a perimeter wall) is a barn with stone steps running up one side, while below is an open cart shed, which is now a garage. More rooms run off the barn at ground level, with old terraces beyond, enclosing hidden gardens resembling town-house courtyards.

ABOVE

A pair of painted and gilded blackamoors appropriately herald the entrance to a formal dining room. The vaulted room, probably an early sheepfold, is the oldest part of the house.

RIGHT

This beautifully made, grand stone arch would have been the main entrance to the farm complex. The house rises above and below the courtyard on several levels, but new stairs and spacious landings now connect all the rooms together.

This property shows off the stonemason's craft at its best. Apart from the traditional timber-beamed ceilings in all the larger rooms, stone is the dominant, and dominating architectural statement. Door- and window frames, arches and gateways, terraces and walls have all been constructed from local stone, collected, shaped and cut in a purposeful and practical manner. There is a quality about the building that indicates a succession of owners of some means, who embellished and maintained the numerous rooms and courtyards with great care.

Like in many Provençal properties today, traditional farming has all but disappeared, and here the massive terraces running east to west across the front of the house have been repaired and rebuilt to contain a breathtaking garden. Further land produces an olive crop, pressed locally for oil, and a large cherry harvest. Though not a true farm, it still has a close relationship with local horticultural and wine producers, who swap equipment, share seasonal tasks and help each other in times of difficulty. Certain skills are kept alive, like the hand-clipping of gigantic cypress columns, performed atop tall ladders with a pair of domestic hedge clippers. This arduous task, often carried out at great speed, is not only undertaken in private gardens but also along highways, and in parks and town centers throughout the south. The coniferous evergreen was usually planted in serried ranks to form a windbreak on the north face of a house, but is now more often used in many gardens to make dramatic vertical statements in garden design. One such plan has used cypress (planted in semicircles, rather than stone or marble columns) as an enclosing feature in a rose garden.

Les Bas Artèmes closely follows the contours of the land, using the dramatic changes of level to great effect. Approached through parkland, the house backs

OPPOSITE & RIGHT

Rustic beamed ceilings in the salon are painted the same pale yellow as the walls in a room that is furnished in a manner that would have astounded the farmers of the past. A beautifully executed watercolor painting of the property hangs opposite a silk-upholstered sofa piled with fine tapestry cushions.

into the landscape and tumbles down the slope towards the south, using the site in the very best manner of climatic protection. Superbly constructed dry-stone walls enclosing carefully chosen plant varieties (those that can bear the bitter winters and blistering summer temperatures) surround even the north facades. Terraces have been built off all the main rooms, yet each one has an enclosed aspect (not overlooked), is south- or west-facing and often completely private. The changes of level are even more apparent inside the house, but good planning has minimized any sense of confusion and the interior decoration is consistent throughout. Soft pastel paintwork, lavish fabrics and richly colored rugs and paintings create a welcoming winter environment, and outdoor "rooms" are used throughout the summer. There is a covered dining terrace for the hottest days, an open area off the kitchen where breakfast is taken on all but the coldest days, and a living and dining complex along the pool terrace. Surrounded by climbing roses and facing southwest is what is called "the sunset platform", a large level area with metal chairs and tables from which to view the seemingly untouched and uninhabited vista beyond.

Although years of work has gone into planning and planting a garden of exceptional color and complexity, the wild natural flora of the region encroaches right to the edge of the manmade composition. A tiny courtyard has been cut into the hillside beside the main bedroom, but a few meters beyond is virgin forest. Here one can clearly hear the sound of water rising up from a natural spring and spilling down the rocky cliff face. That precious resource was probably the reason why the first builders of Les Bas Artèmes chose the site to begin farming.

LEFT & ABOVE

Adjacent to the salon and with views over the valley to the south, the ladies' writing room (which is paneled and painted in a soft aqua) is feminine, decorated with fine eighteenth-century furniture and a floral needlepoint carpet. A fine 18C bust and a pair of crystal claret jugs grace a Provencal chest in the mirrored dining alcove.

LEFT & RIGHT
Steeply pitched, white-painted beamed ceilings in the bedrooms are a counterfoil to the riot of richly colored and patterned fabrics in reds and yellows. The master bedroom has a private walled garden to the side, and an expansive terrace beyond large French doors to the front.

LEFT & ABOVE

Below the house, a sweeping terrace contains an impressively large pool and covered entertaining space with kitchen, changing rooms and showers. The spectacular view encompasses Mont Ventoux in the distance and (left) deep terraces are swathed with roses.

LES BAS ARTÈMES

LEFT & RIGHT

Outside steps were a common feature of old farm buildings. Mostly in shadow, these ancient mossy stones lead to the top of a barn, the lower level of which is now a garage.

BELOW LEFT

Purple-flowered campanula finds sustenance in the dry-stone walls surrounding the house, shown here with steps leading to an ancient trackway linking the hill farms to the valleys below.

Roses scent the air at every turn. Gateposts and terraces, arbors and walkways are smothered in white, cream, pink and golden roses of dazzling variety. The approach to the house is lined with clipped hedges, cypress and a field of old olive trees.

Hundreds of cypress are clipped by hand each year. Once used only as tightly planted wind-breaks, they are now a key vertical statement in modern Provençal gardens.

Uzès

LA BERGERIE DU BOSQUET

Much of Provence is still agricultural and, although crops have changed over the centuries, with fields of lavender replacing wheat and early season vegetables now thriving under hectares of plastic, the pace of the region and look of the landscape are both undoubtedly rural. Mass development has not impinged in areas away from the coast: farmsteads large and small are scattered and often hidden behind trees, in valleys or on terraced hillsides. There is mystery and privacy here; indeed, some travel writers have spoken of feeling like a trespasser. Summer is scorching hot, pushing people indoors; winter can be cold; and the Mistral shuts everything down. Houses rarely advertize themselves - only fortified chateaux and defensive castles rise clearly above the vegetation, sited as they were for clear views of invasion or disturbance.

The term "*bergerie*" is often applied to any secondary dwelling near a house or group of farm buildings, but a true *bergerie* was an important (often skilfully constructed) home for sheep. La Bergerie du Bosquet is in the grand manner of sheepfolds: built in about 1520, when sheep were the most valuable local crop, it had been allowed to decay once the attached farmland had been sold, but the open site with several hectares of land was an attractive proposition for the development of a house and garden. Other ruins indicate a group of farm buildings and their relationship to the *bergerie*.

Typically constructed with dressed-stone arches supported by heavy stone plinths, the building was low and long. Rubble stone walls with tiny slit windows let in minimal light, but the *bergerie's* builder also had an eye for beauty. Along two sides of the building, these original windows have been kept as they were, each space edged with differing-sized, but well-finished stone blocks - a detail usually reserved for men, not animals. Here, the footprint is the same as it was in the 1500s. The outer walls were repaired, and built up with old roof beams found to support a new roof (though covered in antique Roman tiles).

ABOVE & OPPOSITE

The only entrance to this courtyard house and garden is through a large set of curved and painted gates set into a stone wall. Once a barren farmyard, every centimetre of space has been carefully terraced and planted with sweet-smelling herbs and flowers.

The sense of mystery is apparent on the north entrance face - just a blank stone wall with a large carriage-sized wooden door which is slightly pointed at the top and held together with great metal bands - a typical, low-key entrance. There is no visible garden at this point and no idea what lies through the door. A courtyard has been formed as it probably was centuries ago, though now the three built-up sides house the owners and their guests, the great *bergerie* itself filling one side of the rectangle and forming a vast living room. The original compacted-earth floor has been lowered a little, yet the height of the arches and ceilings is not seen from any exterior elevation.

This group of buildings almost huddles in the landscape, never rising above anything around it. The local village rears up above and behind the house, but appears to be leaning backwards, and never seems overbearing or dominant. The buildings face south across what was a gently sloping field and beyond across kilometers of *garrigues*, the aromatic, scrubby heathland common to Provence. Sunflowers dominate the summer landscape and no mountain range can be seen. This is rolling, gentle country - easy to farm, and with abundant water.

The conversion of this purely agricultural building is a good example of sensitive creativity (after all, what's the point of trying to live in ancient buildings if you are going to change the essential style and architecture?). The utter simplicity of the building holds all its charm and, apart from building a large stone fireplace on one wall and covering the ground with limestone blocks laid on sand, very little has changed in nearly 500 years. The walls have been plastered and painted white; the old sheep entrance was retained, although filled with glass-paned doors opening on to the courtyard; and a simple galley kitchen was built across the narrow end of the building. Cool and dimly lit in summer, and warm in winter, this great room exudes age and history - there are no curtains and the space is divided only by groups of furniture. In fact, the room is so large that at one end a dining table, numerous chairs and a very large eighteenth-century painted buffet are almost dwarfed. Capacious sofas face the fire and three more separate "rooms"

On one side of the courtyard is a vast sixteenth-century sheepfold. The walls and massive arches were intact, the floor was just earth, but sensitive restoration has produced a living room of impressive proportion. A simple galley kitchen is tucked into one corner, and (opposite) the dining area is spacious. The room unfolds into several large living rooms by the judicious placing of furniture and rugs in differing groups.

have been formed. At the opposite end to the dining space is a sunken seating area that leads to a secluded graveled terrace. Ottoman embroidery, textiles, pottery and carpets remind one of, if not a seraglio, an exotic and sensuous way to spend summer afternoons.

Interestingly, the old main dwelling was considerably smaller than the *bergerie*. Rebuilt in local stone, the house now looks like many a rural house or farm in southern France. Two-storied, symmetrical, and perfectly in keeping with the other buildings, it links to both *bergerie* and the third range of the courtyard. This centre building is used by the owners as their

private quarters (and is compact and independent from the rest), the guest quarters serve as studio and staff quarters below, while bedrooms with bathrooms and a sitting room fill the upper floor. A typical outdoor stone staircase was built up one wall, and gives on to a small corner terrace reminiscent of a Tuscan farmhouse. The whole is extremely subtle, partly through the superb garden design in the courtyard that links all three buildings. Quite unlike in its agricultural past, the courtyard is planted around a complex pattern of paving using texture, scent and scale. Every window has a view of color and shape; a tiny circular pool has a fountain; and raised beds of lavender and rosemary lead the eye to climbing roses, honeysuckle and wisteria. The field below the house opens out into a series of spaces dominated by two semicircles of pencil-thin cypresses. On a slightly lower level, and hidden until the last minute, are a gracious pool and pavilion.

The use of old local materials, a good understanding of (and sympathy with) agricultural buildings, together with good plantsmanship, have been combined to create a thoroughly modern environment from what was once a ruined sheep farm. Until recently, its buildings were destined to disappear altogether; then a new generation of residents realized the potential of ancient buildings and their ability to adapt with the least structural change possible.

ABOVE & OPPOSITE

The original barn doors have been replaced with glass and small windows inserted into the thick stone walls in the dining area, but little light penetrates into the voluminous, cool space. A massive stone fireplace (above right), its scale in keeping with the size of the room, was added during renovation work, along with new, almost white, stone floors. The furnishings are largely French, chosen for shape and large scale, as a room of this size would simply dwarf contemporary pieces.

Ruined farm buildings have been rebuilt opposite the barn. A light-filled summer studio fills the ground floor, while guest bedrooms, bathroom and sitting room are colorful and exuberant. The red and white fabric on the walls is an overscaled embroidery design, the quilt is an English antique, and the bed is nineteenth-century French ironwork.

ABOVE RIGHT

A writing desk is set before a guest-room window overlooking the central courtyard. Planted with scented roses and herbs, and with a cooling fountain in the center, the courtyard links all three sides of the house. The local village rises above the central section of the house on the left, which contains further bedrooms and a large concealed roof terrace.

ABOVE & RIGHT

One of several, tiny original openings in the barn wall. Pergola covered seating areas abound and, in such a sheltered setting, meals are taken outdoors most of the year.

OPPOSITE

Approached by stone steps on the outside of the building, the entrance to the guest quarters is slightly Italianate in its design. The ground slopes away gently to the left, revealing a wondrous, Ottoman-inspired garden, created in the sheep pastures below the house.

ABOVE

The secret garden paved with a calcade, a pebbled pathway whose design was inspired by the Topkapi palace in Istanbul. In fact, much of the garden design was developed around the work of the famous Ottoman architect Sinan, and built in stages over several years. Each window has its own special view. There are hidden areas to explore, and a superb mix of textures – both natural and clipped – relying on leaf shape and form rather than color.

OPPOSITE

Two semicircles of pencil-thin cypress mark out lavender beds above the swimming pool, set at a slightly lower level. Rose arches form gateways between each section of the garden, where color is limited to a palette of green, grey, silver, mauve and white highlighted by pink. Potted citrus trees and old olives mix with verbena and rock roses around the gracious pool.

Paradou

LES MAS DE L'ESQUIÈRES

The view from this long, narrow farmhouse leads the eye right to Marseille, or that is how it feels. Without a single sign of human habitation, apart from a pair of Moorish watchtowers dwarfed to the size of toys on a far hill, much of the region's flora can be seen in one sweeping panorama and, best of all, a large field of lavender drops away at one's feet down the hill like a swathe of purple silk. Probably built by a farmer in the late eighteenth century, the (then) very small house began life as an almost square, two-storied dwelling, housing people, crops and perhaps some animals on the earth floor at ground level.

Tucked up against a rock face for maximum shelter, the house has been added to over decades, maybe centuries, along a now level, manmade terrace that today forms the main outdoor living area. Towering pines and ancient terraces create an atmosphere more reminiscent of the higher altitudes of the Montagne du Lubéron, but this is still olive-growing country and old trees can be found all over the property. The view to the south comprises numerous shades of green, grey and purple, yet the hills behind are stark and bare (and in places pure white), sculptural in form and intensely interesting to geologists.

It is likely the builder used a mixture of stone from older buildings nearby or picked up quantities of loose stone from the surrounding land. There is a very long tradition of recycling building materials in Provence, evidenced by the number of stone blocks quarried and shaped by the early Greeks. These are often found in Roman ruins, and Roman building blocks are still seen in many towns and villages, though it takes an expert eye to determine the age and provenance of such valuable materials. Apart from one wall, in what forms a courtyard at the rear, the whole house is built of roughly pointed stone. What is now the tallest inside courtyard facade of the old house has been plastered and painted cerulean blue - rather more typical of a Greek island, with its pure white shutters, but as this is a private seating area, never seen from the front, it is a colourful surprise, and especially pleasant in winter. Across the long south front, windows and doors that are larger than the original openings have been cut through the great thickness of wall to allow light - and air - to flow in from back to front. There is no symmetrical design - the roof heights vary, as do the window and door sizes - yet there is a pleasing sense of facade, linked by blue-green painted shutters and the loose planting of roses and plumbago tucked behind a tightly clipped lavender hedge.

Almost all Provençal outdoor surfaces - forming paths, driveways, dining areas and terraces - are covered with a layer of pea-sized limestone gravel. This free-draining material is ideally suited to hard surfaces, and of course the colour nearly always matches the stone of the surrounding barns, houses and garden statuary. There is also a pleasing softness underfoot - no heavy crunching sounds and, because it is usually such a thinly spread surface, high heels are not instantly shredded. The wide gravel terrace running the full width of the house is really just a smarter extension of the stony track that leads up to the house from a narrow road below. The terrace extends to a traditionally reed-covered permanent seating area, with a fully equipped "summer" kitchen attached. Some residents boast of family Christmas lunches outdoors, although January and February are probably

the months to light the fire and come indoors. Slightly higher up, on another old terrace, a swimming pool sits above the roof height of the main bedroom below.

Unlike many larger houses, and because it was extended sideways, there are virtually no corridors linking rooms. The tall end of the house has been converted into bedrooms and bathrooms on both levels and incorporates a simple, curved staircase that gives access to the kitchen and courtyard. Built of stone originally, the stair risers were later plastered and painted the same ochre wash as two of the kitchen walls. The steps, however, have been covered in old terracotta tiles, which have been used throughout the house in slightly differing shapes and sizes. Off the kitchen is a dining area, completely open to the large sitting room that forms the physical and social centre of the house. The tall, beamed ceilings are painted the same milky white as the walls and the plastered fireplace in the centre.

Even though the dining area backs on to the rock wall behind, it is never dark, since light from the blue courtyard to one side floods in through large, glass doors. Filled with comfortable old sofas and chairs, almost every surface is decorated with Asian textiles, collected in Laos, Burma, Hong Kong and China - a haphazard but complementary mix of color and texture that works so well within a simple farmhouse interior. A pair of old doors either side of the fireplace leads on

A faultless Provençal vignette - mixed summer planting, edged with a lavender hedge, glows in bright sunshine along the front of an old mas. *White plumbago teamed with a pink rose is styled perfectly with the "wheelbarrow" colored shutters.*

one side to a large storage area lit by roof lights; on the other, the doors lead (at first glance) to an office, and it is only the fax, computer and printer set up on an old Chinese table that indicate a workspace. A magnificent antique bed, draped in silks and embroidered cushions, more or less fills the room.

Right at the end, under an enormous central beam that would easily support a floor above, is the master bedroom and bathroom. Like every room in the house, it has its own door to the terrace, but this was probably originally built just for farm storage. The rough-stone walls and beamed ceiling have been painted pure white - the only decoration (if one can call it that) needed to transform an old shed into a Provençal bedroom.

Very little alteration has taken place since Les Mas de l'Esquières was built and extended, and the house is a good example of how well old agricultural buildings, with the least interference, adapt to modern use. Early builders clearly understood the elements and the needs of living and working in a single group of buildings. Stone, timber and tile - local materials worked by local people - have lasted the distance.

ABOVE & OPPOSITE

As the house is essentially only one room wide, the rooms flow one after the other, each with doors into the garden. Several plate glass windows were replaced to match the original smaller-paned variety. Fortunately, the floor tiles - in various soft ochre shades - were extant. The decoration relies on richly colored textiles, many collected in Laos and other parts of the East.

ABOVE & OPPOSITE

Rough stone walls have been left unplastered in the kitchen. Although fully equipped, it is seldom used during the summer as a further kitchen has been built beside the outdoor dining room near the pool. The soft terracotta wash on the walls extends to the inner hall and staircase leading to bedrooms on the first floor, while the cupboards are painted a similar grey-green to the shutters hung at all the windows across the front of the house. Adjacent to the kitchen is a large, open-plan dining room, slightly raised by one step above the salon.

The window off the kitchen looks on to the blue courtyard at the back of the house, and the stairs lead to bedrooms on the upper floor. Further bedrooms have been created on the ground floor of what may have been the original mill.

The master bedroom is at the opposite end of the house. From the outside it appears hardly tall enough to stand up in and was originally a chicken house or animal shelter. The rough-stone wall, beams and ceiling have been painted in a pure, bright white, which creates a romantic retreat when teamed with shades of blue.

ABOVE & OPPOSITE

Protected on three sides by the house and the cliff face on the fourth, this vivid blue courtyard emerges as a complete surprise, seen only from the windows at the back of kitchen and sitting room. Furnished almost like a room, with a mosaic-topped table, iron chairs and day bed softened with bright cotton cushions and Chinese ceramic stools, the space is a true extension to the house.

LEFT & ABOVE

As much a viewing platform as a summer dining room, the cane-covered, raised terrace is a magnet
for all ages. There is an uninterrupted view all the way to Marseille across rolling terraces of lavender,
and close by is the swimming pool set on a higher level and surrounded by pine forest. Rendered
concrete seating is covered with striped cushions and Moroccan lanterns are lit in the evenings.

LE MURIER

Le Murier, in hameau des Auvis, is situated close enough to Uzès for some local people still to walk to the market. Quiet narrow roads following old tracks lead one past vines, cherry orchards, asparagus fields and giant sunflowers, although earlier economic prosperity was gained through the manufacture of linen, serge and silk. A late nineteenth-century photograph, taken straight along the street, shows that in more than 500 years nothing appears to have changed here at all.

Being neither village nor farm, the French *hameau* (hamlet) comprises a group of houses and barns, cottages, stables, and often a *pigeonnier*, all of which were interrelated and often co-dependent. In essence this was a miniature, feudal society reliant on the land for a living and where each family contributed its own special skills. The landowner sometimes lived in the "big" house, but frequently had another residence elsewhere and spent time during the summer harvest, or holidays, on his land. Everybody else lived and worked on the property and shared much of the year's work. Important seasonal tasks like picking fruit, the grape harvest and the olive harvest were shared tasks, as were making bread, growing vegetables and hunting game, which were as important as the business of farming. Provence is justly famous for its many quaint and well-preserved *hameaus*. Often situated in the rich and fertile lowlands, defence was not a major consideration when building. More important were easy access to markets and a reliable source of water, as this type of farming was thought quite intensive in its day.

This sense of a tiny village is enhanced by the fact that there is a central street off which all the elements of the *hameau* lead. There are no footpaths, so all doors and barns open straight on to the street. Beaded or cane curtains are frequently to be seen across the front door, allowing air into the house but still providing privacy. All the houses have shutters in a wide variety of colours, from faded claret to several shades of blue and an intense lavender. A great deal of thought and concern goes into the choice of color, since it is often the only individual mark that can be displayed externally. The debate rages about the correct one to use, but there seems to be a preponderance of silvery olive green here.

At one end of the street a pair of majestic, stone gateposts supporting a fine wrought-iron gate announces the importance of the dwelling beyond. There is very little garden, though just enough for tables and chairs to be set on the grass under enormous old trees. This is the "big" house, and opposite are barns (likely to have once housed the owner's carriage) and a field of fruit trees. Further along begins the mixture of rough-stone dwellings that are now all private homes, but at one time these would perhaps have served the estate as a forge, bread oven, kennels and poultry houses, as well as farm workers' cottages. Towards the other end are two noticeably larger, detached houses, one much older and simpler than the other. Possibly built by tenant farmers after good crops, there are details such as a carved stone lintel over a doorway, which indicate more status and wealth than the attached cottages could match.

As is usual in an area of severe planning restrictions, Le Murier was restored without altering the original dwelling's layout, although the first floor was probably raised at some point in the past. From the front, only the kitchen window and entrance door on the ground floor and two bedroom windows above are visible, though the house is far more spacious that the stone facade would indicate. Off the entrance hall is the kitchen, including the old fireplace, which was used for both cooking and warmth. Although modernized, it has been kept deliberately simple and retains a useful old built-in cupboard as well as freestanding furniture painted in rustic Provençal style. A farmhouse table and folding chairs allow the occupants to chat through the kitchen window to passing neighbors, the bread-delivery man, the postman... Some walls have been plastered, while others have been left exactly as they were found. The local stone is particularly pale - a most-sought-after and currently fashionable shade of white. Exposed supporting beams have been left unpainted across the ceiling in the sitting room, but in the bedrooms the interiors are white. Furnishings are restricted to worn and well-used pieces, mostly found locally and painted. Immensely thick stone walls divide up the rear section of the ground floor, but the back wall has been broken through and enlarged, allowing access to a tiny walled garden.

No matter how small, gardens provide a valuable living space throughout the summer, and all over Provence massive, stone-topped tables are permanently placed in a shady area for dining during the day or at night. In *A Year in Provence*, Peter Mayle first drew attention to the logistical struggle of having one of

ABOVE

A silvery green shuttered kitchen window typically opens
straight on to the street in country villages. The choice of
paint color varies here from vivid lavender to ox-blood red and
every known shade of blue and green.

these essential monsters of outdoor furniture installed,
yet nearly every house has one, old or new. Larger
gardens often have major fountains, pools or channels
of running water, but even in the tiniest garden the
sound of running water is cooling and can just consist
of an old lead pipe, curved at the end with a mask
behind attaching it to a stone basin. Water was (and

still is, during a drought) the most precious commodity
in this community, soothing mind and body, and
nurturing ever more intensive agriculture.

While an *hameau* may not adhere to any particular
architectural style, it is the very irregularity of its size
and shape, roofline and door, and its openness to the
surrounding countryside, that is recognizable from
afar. One has a heightened sense of expectation when
coming across such a semi-private group of buildings
that together have public access and a long history of
continuity. Will there be a grand *bastide* (country
house) through the tall trees, perhaps; a derelict farm
to explore; or (even better) a restored cottage for sale?

ABOVE

This simply furnished dining room leads off an inner hall and out into the walled garden. Natural timber beams and powdery white paint set the style for decoration both here and in the sitting room, to the right of the hall.

OPPOSITE

The old fireplace would have been used for cooking and heating, but now acts as useful storage space for wine and water. The cupboards on the left, original to the house, have been painted the same color as the shutters.

OPPOSITE & BELOW LEFT

Mesh panels and vivid paintwork distinguish a cupboard intended for a dairy. Provençal kitchens were never fitted, but rather furnished with dressers, shelves and hardy wooden cupboards that could withstand constant use. The painted panel of a woman in traditional costume has been stuck on to the door leading to the dining room.

ABOVE RIGHT

A gloriously painted symbol of France, the model chicken stands beside a straw shopping basket, something that is found in every Provençal home and available in markets throughout the country. Baskets often become well-used collections of old friends, and come in numerous shapes and sizes – some with leather handles, some open-weave – and are used constantly for bringing fresh produce, eggs or indeed live chickens, home to local kitchens.

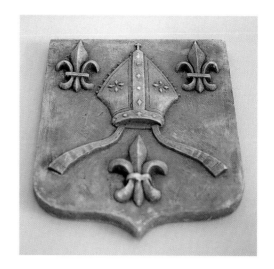

LEFT

Lit only by a fanlight above the front door, the wide entrance hall is surprisingly light. A nineteenth-century bust, greets visitors The central staircase leads to the guest bedrooms and a roof terrace.

ABOVE

The Papal symbol of Avignon is one of a collection of plaster casts hung in a group in the hall. The ram's head is North African but is a common Provençal motif, often adorning clay and stone pots.

Two guest rooms, decorated in shades of white, cream and grey-blue, face the street. The master bedroom is at the back of the house, tucked into the sloping roof. Varying rooflines and wall heights are common in these old houses, where much of the original structure was intended for agricultural use rather than living rooms. Old painted shutters are used as a headboard (opposite), their faded grey paintwork toning perfectly with the adjacent portrait. The house is simply furnished with pieces chosen for their good shape and color, and especially for original paint, no matter whether flaking or worn.

OPPOSITE & ABOVE

A single, enormous tree acting as an umbrella shades the enclosed garden. Hugging the stone walls are massed

plantings of hydrangea mixed with clipped, potted box and petunias. A tiny fountain trickles in one corner,

and beyond the wall is an orchard and open farmland.

INDEX

Page numbers in *italics* refer to captions/illustrations

Aix-en-Provence 29, 31
    Pavillon de Victoire *62*, *63–6*, *64–79*
alleyways *49*
Alpes Maritimes 9, 13, 103
Alpilles *137*
aqueducts, Roman 104
arches *156*, *171*
Argens, River 103, *141*
Arles 9, 28, 29–31, 31, *32–45*
armoire *106*
Arnold, Chester *149*
art *144*, *147*, *149*, 209
    animal paintings *73*
    botanical prints *109*
    chalk drawings *66*
    painted panel *205*
    rural scenes *24*
    watercolor of property *159*
Avignon 29, 31
Avignon, Archbishop of 63

balconies *17*, 30, *101*
bar, zinc-topped *124*, *127*
barns *155*, *176*, *181*, 200
Les Bas Artèmes, near Menerbes *154–69*, *155–9*
baskets *205*
Basses-Alpes 103
bathrooms *55*, *66*, *75*, *82*, *96*, *149*
bedcovers, Thai silk *41*
bedrooms *27*, *41*, *55*, *66*, *95*, *114*, *124–5*, *131*, *139*, *141*, *150*, *162*, *179*, *187*, *193*, 209
beds *27*, *114*, *131*, *141*, *179*, *187*
bell tower *99*
bells, door *79*
benches, Anglo-Chinese *79*
La Bergerie du Bosquet, Uzès *170–83*, *171–5*
Besse-sur-Issole 103

blackamoors *156*
Bonnieux *47*
bookcases, carved *36*
Bouches-du-Rhône 103
Brauerman, Sylvia *113*
breakfast room *141*
Brignoles 103

calcade *182*
candlesticks *34*, *90*
Carnoules *102*, *103–5*, *105–19*
Carpentras *63*
carpets *66*, *75*, *110*, *161*
cave (winery) 104, *106*
ceilings:
    beamed *27*, *33*, *82*, *124*, *139*, *156*, *159*, *162*, *186*, *200*, *202*
    painted timber 30
Chabin, E. *144*
chairs:
    American Arts and Crafts *82*, *89*
    café *125*, *132*
    caned *68*
    contemporary *144*
    country *24*
    court *128*
    English *150*
    fauteuils *90*
    folding 200
    Hepplewhite *105*
    iron *194*
    Italian *68*
    Louis XVII *86*
    painted 30, *65*, *68*
    priests' *41*
    Regency-style *90*
    zebra *52*
chaises longues *147*
chest of drawers *149*
chinoiserie *65*, *68*
cinema room *82*, *95*
commode *105*
copperware *89*
courtyards *159*, *172*, *175*, *193*, *194*
    entrance *48*, *56*

interior 30, *44*, *106*, *179*, *185–6*
cupboards *110*, *202*, *205*
cypresses *101*, *134*, *156*, *169*, *175*, *182*

daybeds *82*, *95*, *125*, *132*, *194*
defence, ring of houses for 13–14
dining rooms 23, *68*, *82*, *86*, *105*, *109*, *110*, *113*, *124*, *127*, *139*, *155*, *202*
    open-plan *190*
    outdoor *190*, *197*
dog beds, built-in *66*, *89*
Domaine du Grand Cros, Carnoules *102* *103–5*, *105–19*
door knockers *85*
door-frames, stone *68*, *156*
doors:
    bead curtains on *199*
    carriage-sized *172*
    double *33*, *65*
    fabric-lined *65*, *68*
    French *17*, *18*, *90*, 104, *110*, *113*, *162*
    glass *176*, *186*
    hessian-covered *128*
    interconnecting between houses 14
    rustic *17*
doorways, blocked *48*
drawing rooms 30, *105*, *113*, *124*, *141*, *144*
dressers *24*, *127*
drives, river-gravel *65*

entrance halls *85*, *106*, 207

fabrics:
    Asian *186*, *188*
    Belgian linen *73*, *90*
    Bracquénie *75*
    French cotton *75*
    hessian sackcloth *124*
    on walls *179*
    white- and woad-dyed linen *105*
fig trees *81*, *99*
fireplaces 8, *17*, 31, *38*, *89*, *95*, *110*, *131*, *143*, *172*, *176*, 200, *202*
flagstones *81–2*, *85*, *86*
floors:

earth *124*
    limestone *48*, *81–2*, *172*
    oak *82*, *95*
    stone 8, *124*, *176*
fountains *56*, *79*, *82*, *95*, *139*, *201*, *211*
Fréjus 103
frieze, bas-relief *143*

gardens 104, *117*, *124*, *125*, *132*, *134*, *139*, *156*, *169*, *181*, *182*, *200–1*
    courtyard *172*, *175*
    formal *65*, *66*, *77*, *80*, *82–3*, *83*, *101*
    hidden *155*, *182*
    walled 200, *211*
garrigues *172*
gates *77*, *134*, *139*, *172*, 200
gateways, stone *48*, *139*, *139*, 200
Georgiou, Elpida *141*
glassware 30, *34*, *161*
Gordes 13, *47*
Grasse 13
gravel *186*
grille, carved *128*

Hadjiganev, Albert *147*
halls:
    entrance *85*, *106*, 207
    inner *109*, *139*
hameau *198–201*
holly, clipped *63*, *65*
Hyères 103

ironwork 8, *82*, *85*, *114*
Issole, River 103

jars, Chinese *106*

Kismet, Arles 28, 29–31, 31, *32–45*
kitchens 20, 30, *34*, *49*, *51*, *65–6*, *70*, *82*, *89*, *127*, *190*, 200, *205*
    galley *172*, *175*
    open-plan *139*, *141*
    outdoor *139*, *150*, *165*, *186*, *190*
Kohlmayer, Ida *147*

Lacoste 47, 122, 123-5, 125-35
ladies' writing room 161
lakes 124
latches 8, 23, 82, 114
libraries 82, 124, 131
lighting:
    candle lanterns 132
    ceiling 95
    draped 49
    lamps 147
    Moroccan lanterns 197
living rooms 139, 141, 172-5, 175, 176
Luberon 46, 47-9, 49, 50-9
Lubéron, Montagne de 185
Luberon Garden 123, 134

Les Maccans, Lacoste 122, 123-5, 125-35
marble 96
Marseille 29
Les Mas de l'Esquières, Paradou 184-5, 185-7, 187-97
Les Mas du Grès, St Rémy-de-Provence 80, 81-3, 83-101
Mas du Manescau, St-Rémy-de-Provence 136-7, 137-41, 138, 140, 141, 142-53
mats, straw 128
Mayle, Peter 200
meadow, wild-flower 139
Menerbes 47, 154-69, 155-9
mezzanine floors 48, 52, 124, 131
mirrors 19, 75, 110
Mistral 8
Mongolian tent lining 41
Mougins 12, 13-15, 15, 16-27
Le Murier, Uzès 198-9, 199-201, 201-11

Nostradamus 137

olives 103, 156, 169, 182, 185
Order of St Augustine 29

Paradou 184-5, 185-7, 187-97
paths, pebble 124, 134, 182
Pavillon de Victoire, Aix-en-Provence 62, 63-6, 64-79

pergola 181
planters, lead 89
plaster casts 207
Plateau des Antiques 137
ponds/pools 79, 83, 139, 153, 165, 182, 201
pots 42, 63, 143, 144
Provence:
    architecture 8-9
    boundaries 8

quilts 82, 95, 124, 125, 179

radassière 95
Raynaud, Aurélien 73
reception rooms 30, 31
Renfrow, Greg 141
Riviera 13
rock, houses built into 13-14, 23, 48
Romans 9
roof terraces 14-15, 48, 52, 56, 179
roofs, tile 105, 171
Rousseau, Jean-Jacques 65
rugs 52, 147

Sade, Marquis de 123
St Paul de Mausole 137
St-Rémy-de-Provence:
    Mas du Grès 80, 81-3, 83-101
    Mas du Manescau 136-7, 137-41, 138, 140, 141, 142-53
St Tropez 103
salons 36, 38, 52, 66, 68, 82, 86, 139
Saracens 47
screens, ironwork 114
sculpture 153
seating, concrete 197
sheepfolds 171, 175
shutters 15, 30, 31, 36, 124, 137, 150, 190, 199-200, 201
    as headboard 209
sinks, stone 51, 65, 70
sitting rooms 48, 52, 55, 66, 73, 124, 127, 128, 131
sofas 36, 113, 124, 131, 144, 159, 172
stable 47-8

staircases 109, 149, 207
    ironwork handrails 82, 92
    spiral 14, 30
    stone 30, 33, 44, 63, 65, 68, 82, 92, 124
    exterior 48, 167, 175
    tiled 186
    timber 48, 52, 82, 86
statuary 63, 66, 207
steps, stone 167
stone, recycling 185
stools, ceramic 194
Stringer, Jim 153
study 139
swimming pools 85, 125, 134, 155, 186, 197

tables:
    console 90, 144
    dining 30, 34, 105
    draper's 30, 34
    farmhouse 200
    hexagonal 90
    marble-topped 110
    with Masonic symbols 65, 68
    mosaic-topped 194
    oak and slate 82, 89
    scagliola 30, 38
    side- 141
    stone-topped 200-1
    teak 125
    tree trunk 150
Tarlow, Rose 90
terraces 30, 42, 82, 85, 90, 95, 113, 125, 132, 134, 139, 155, 159, 185
    covered 124, 159
    front 104, 139, 139, 156, 162
    grassy 123
    gravel 77, 186
    pool 153, 165, 186
    raised 197
    roof 14-15, 48, 52, 56, 179
Thompson, Jim 41
tiles 17, 66, 82, 186, 188
tomb guardians, Ming 38
topiary 66, 85, 99
Toulon 103

trellis 30, 34, 150
troughs, feeding 104, 117

Uzès:
Le Bergerie du Bosquet 170-83, 171-5
Le Murier 198-9, 199-201, 201-11

Van Gogh, Vincent 137
Var 103
Vaucluse 103
Ventoux, Mont 165
Verey, Charles 150
Via Domitia 47
villages, fortified 47

walls:
    dry-stone 125, 159, 167
    exterior 105
    limestone 48
    stone 33, 123, 171, 190
    stripped 52
water garden 83, 99
wells 99, 139, 153
Wendling, Anne 153
windows:
    double-height 85
    French windows/doors 17, 18, 90, 104, 110, 113, 162
    full-height 66
    glass wall 49, 51, 139
    latches for 8, 23
    plants in and around 31, 187
    slit 171
    stained-glass 30, 33
wines 103, 104
writing desk 179

Year in Provence 200
yew, clipped 63

ACKNOWLEDGMENTS

We would like to extend grateful thanks to the owners of the houses featured in this book, for both their patience and their hospitality. Listed below are those who agreed to be named and others who provided invaluable help while the authors were in France.

LANDSCAPE ENTERPRISE LTD
Rue Basse
Lacoste 84480
Tel 00 33 490 75 86 34
Fax 00 33 490 75 88 09
e-mail alex@admgarden.com

Alex Dingwall-Main, Garden architect and designer. Author of the Lubéron Garden (2002), and The Angel Tree(2003) Ebury Press. (pages 122 to 135)

FRENCH COUNTRY LIVING
21, Rue De L'Eglise
Mougins 06250
Tel 00 33 493 75 53 03

Douglas and Jean Hill, antiques dealers specialising in French and Italian furniture often with original paintwork - decorative items, mirrors and old linens. (pages 12 to 27)

DECORACION ET JARDINS
3, Place des Trois Ormeaux
Aix-en-Provence 13100
Tel 00 33 442 35232

Jean-Louis Raynaud and Kenyon Kramer. International interior and garden designers. House and garden on pages 62 to 79 see also Les Mas du Grès on pages 80 to 101 and Les Bas Artèmes on pages 154 to 169

DAVID PRICE
Mas des Chataigniers
Chemin du Grava
Le Paradou 13520 - near St. Rémy-de-Provence
Tel 00 33 490 54 30 04
e-mail aprice@club-internet.fr

David Price - Architectural building and renovation business for international clients throughout Provence. Expert on sourcing local materials and reclaimed items, interior planning/design and high quality finishes. (not illustrated himself - see Robert Hering and Jim Stringer Mas de Manescau on pages 136 to 153

DOMAINE DU GRAND CROS
Rte de Carnoules 83890
Besse-sur-Issole
Var
Tel 00 33 498 01 80 08
e-mail jhf@grandcros.fr

Hon Hugh J. Jane and Julian Faulkner - Winemakers (pages 102 to 117)

BRUNO & ALEXANDRE LAFOURCADE
Bureau D'Etudes
10, Boulevard Victor Hugo
Saint-Rémy-de-Provence 13210
Tel 00 33 490 92 10 14
Fax 00 33 490 92 49 72

Bruno Lafourcade - Architecture and design studio specialising in all areas of traditional Provençal country house renovation, re-design and building. Dominic Lafourcade, garden designer and artist.

Barbara Ther (pages 198 to 211)
Les Muriers
Uzes

Robert Hering and Jim Stringer (pages 136 to 153)
Mas du Manescau
Saint-Rémy-du-Provence

LES MAS DES GRES
Hotel de charme
Route d'Apt RN 100
F-84800 Lagnes near l'Isle-sur-la-Sorgue
Tel 00 33 490 20 21 45
Fax 00 33 490 20 21 45
e-mail info@masdesgres.com

Nina & Thierry Crovara, the best kitchen in Vaucluse.

TIM REES AND BRITA VON SCHOENAICH
149 Liverpool Road
London N1 0RF
Tel 00 44 207 837 3800

Major garden design, construction and planting undertaken throughout Provence.

ROBERT DALLAS
Cabinet d'architecture
Domaine de Notre Dame
06570 Saint-Paul-de-Vence
Tel 00 33 494 32 55 55
e-mail rd@dallas.com

Robert Hering artwork credits:

LIVING ROOM
"Series Squares" by Ida Kohlmayer

BEDROOM - ABOVE BED
"Sunrise" by Michael Daly

BEDROOM - ABOVE CHAISE
"Cote Normande" by Albert Hadjiganev

PICTURE ABOVE CONSOLE TABLE
"L'Enchanteresse" by E. Chabin

PICTURE ABOVE CHEST IN INNER HALL
"Elegies 2" by Chester Arnold

KITCHEN ABOVE REFRIGERATOR (IN ROOF PEAK)
Untitled by Greg Renfrow

DINING AREA
"Boxer Shorts" by Elpida Georgiou

KITCHEN (TO LEFT OF FIREPLACE)
"Come Un Paesaggio Urbano" by M Marzo